W9-CHQ-816

MORE PRAISE FOR *THE NEW GAME CHANGERS*

"*The New Game Changers* is a compelling story with innovative and inspiring ideas. Long and Newman's TOPS model reveals that the standard way of doing business is not necessarily the path to a winning outcome. Their model is useful for all businesspeople and for anyone who is trying to help a group of people improve their performance."
— *Christopher Rice, President, BlessingWhite, and coauthor of* The Engagement Equation

"Butler and Greg have been involved in human performance improvement for over twenty-five years, in hundreds of settings around the globe. They are both relentless learners, and they have compiled an invaluable summary of their many lessons learned over the years. More important, they have developed a practical, straightforward system that will help any organization move swiftly to unlock operational excellence."
— *John Beakes, cofounder and COO, RWD Technologies*

"*The New Game Changers* brings to life a real-world situation I would bet most people have seen. Follow Aimee's wild ride into selling internally as well as externally. Outcome selling using the TOPS checklist is an often-overlooked way to make a good sales team a great sales team. This approach reminds me of Ben Franklin's comment 'involve me and I will learn.' If you read this, you will understand what he means."
— *Chris Chitterling, National Account Director, US technology company*

"A must-read for any business leader, *The New Game Changers* is engaging and delightful in illustrating how to best leverage frontline performers to improve a company's bottom-line performance."
— *Ken Rebeck, President, KRA Associates, LLC*

"This book is an easy read and a practical illustration of how to maximize your greatest asset—people. The way the story unfolds allows you to imagine how you can use Outcomes Thinking to maximize performance in virtually any situation to drive your business forward."
— *Gary Walker, cofounder, InteCrowd*

"Firms spend countless dollars seeking answers to their people performance challenges. Every firm has top performers, and the answer lies within. The road map to finding that answer lies within this book. With twenty-five years of experience in relationship management and developing relationship managers, I've read lots of books on the subject. Few add anything new, fewer focus on results, and fewer still offer practical advice, applicable to every team. This book does all these."

— Kevin Boyle CFA, Head of Private Wealth
Management, Fitch Learning

"An incredibly well-done job. I never would have imagined it would make me not want to put it down. While it's partly my affinity for the subject matter, the unfolding of the story is really well done. The message comes across very well, and the football analogy helps significantly. The tool kit at the end is also balanced nicely."

— Rick Contel, independent performance consultant

"*The New Game Changers* uses a novel narrative format with real-world examples of the challenges every business struggles with, while providing an outcome-driven framework for success."

— Christopher Lane, Vice President of Engineering and
Technology, top ten market television station

"Long and Newman nailed it. An orientation toward outcomes-based thinking creates a pathway toward the clarity, focus, and impact that all organizations need to thrive. This is a straightforward, immediately usable approach that can help leaders transform business results. This goes on the must-read list for leaders at all levels."

— Andrew Freedman, Principal, entreQuest

*Paul /
To a fellow
Game Changer*

The New Game Changers

Driving Performance
by Focusing on What Matters

⋮

Greg

Greg Long
Butler Newman

THIRD BRIDGE PRESS

Third Bridge Press
839 Bestgate Road, #400
Annapolis, MD 21401
www.thirdbridgepress.com

Quantity sales. Special discounts are available on quantity purchases by corporations, associations, and others. For details, contact the "Special Sales Department" at the address above.

Orders by US trade bookstores and wholesalers. Please contact BCH: (800) 431-1579 or visit www.bookch.com for details.

Printed in the United States of America

Long, Greg,
        The new game changers: driving performance by focusing on what matters / Greg Long, Butler Newman. —
First edition.
    pages cm
        LCCN 2015933991
    ISBN 978-0-9862531-0-2 (hardback)
    ISBN 978-0-9862531-1-9 (ebook)

    1. Leadership. 2. Success in business. I. Newman, Butler. II. Title.
HD57.7.L662015   658.4'092
QBI15-600059

19 18 17 16 15   10 9 8 7 6 5 4 3 2 1

To our wives, Lyn and Jill.

Contents

A Game-Changing Approach

It's about getting things down to results.

That's the key insight Jonah Hill's character, Peter Brand, had in the popular 2011 movie *Moneyball*. Brand was trying to figure out how the Oakland A's could capture a winning season without the benefit of big-name talent, but he might as well have been talking about the challenge facing any business today.

That challenge, simply stated, is this: there is not enough top talent to go around, so how do we get good, solid people to produce great results? The challenge is further complicated as companies inadvertently and incorrectly marginalize the importance of the front line by focusing instead on technology. It doesn't matter if companies are regionally or globally focused: if they hope to win in today's complex business environment, their frontline workers must perform consistently at or above standards. If they want to leapfrog the competition, companies must figure out how to develop leadership teams and frontline performers who are focused on the vital actions that actually drive the business.

But how best to do that? A solution is urgently needed. Today's corporations are dynamic environments in which leaders come and go, bottom-line pressures force us to think in the short term, and the next new idea on how to save the company is always right around the corner. Technological advances change the competitive environment and demand our attention. Old alliances fade. People are viewed as unimportant. And if it can be digitized, disaggregated, and automated, the prevailing thought is that it should be. It seems that new strategies, tools, and pressures occupy every bit of available white space in today's organizations. The clutter is suffocating, and in the deluge, the few ideas that can truly have impact are drowned out by the constant noise of the new.

We have written this book to introduce a different type of solution to this underlying and basic issue facing all companies today: creating and maintaining predictable, high levels of frontline performance.

Our approach is based on thirty years of trial and error, on the research and practices of a small group of individuals who have been committed to performance of the front line, and on, quite frankly, years of asking the wrong questions, such as "What do people need to know?" "How do I engage the learners?" and "How do I modernize and mobilize my learning programs?" These are not bad questions, but they have not yielded the answers that really matter. Instead, we first have to ask a much more fundamental question: *What specific outcomes do I want my frontline performers to produce?*

Answering this question requires a shift of perspective; it requires a small but significant quarter turn in thinking about how to describe and focus the development of frontline performers. We call the approach that results from this quarter turn *Outcomes Thinking*.

Outcomes Thinking is a game-changing strategy. Let's go back to the baseball analogy for a moment. The insight of the Peter Brand character was to study baseball players' outcomes rather than their physical profile, their perceived potential, or even their competencies. "Your goal shouldn't be to buy players. Your goal should be to buy wins," Brand says during a pivotal scene in *Moneyball*. To win, a baseball team needs to score runs. When the team started focusing on runs and how individual players could be deployed to get them, the Oakland A's in the movie, just like the team in real life, transformed from a small-market team into a franchise that could compete with multimillion-dollar franchises like the New York Yankees and the Boston Red Sox.

But how does Outcomes Thinking translate from the baseball diamond to the boardroom? When properly deployed, Outcomes Thinking not only tackles the tough problem of frontline performance but also informs other important areas, such as recruiting, job design, capabilities, and learner engagement.

From the front line to the back office, our experience in putting Outcomes Thinking into practice has been both surprising and gratifying. When this new approach has been implemented, employees often let out an almost audible sigh that speaks volumes: "Finally, those people at corporate get it. They understand my job and are now providing me with real tools, training, and coaching to help me perform it better." We have worked with hundreds of individuals in numerous companies over the past thirty years, helping each of them, in their own way, achieve this amazingly gratifying result.

Like most powerful ideas, Outcomes Thinking itself is simple and straightforward, but putting it into practice can be a challenge. Implementing and adopting the idea across an organization can get "lost in the noise" of too many competing initiatives and the unending distractions found in modern organizations. Moving an idea forward against all of that corporate noise requires grit and focus. It takes both an inquisitive mind and determination—sometimes lots of determination—as well as a vision for how it should play out. As Albert Einstein said, "Example isn't another way to teach, it is the only way to teach."

With that in mind, we offer you a story of one person's quest to discover the secret of performance—an example of how a focused individual can marshal a group's performance to achieve the kinds of results that impact business.

Although the situation, the company, and the characters are fictional, we have drawn on many real-life experiences to create a story that condenses, but does not exaggerate, the "noise" found in companies today. And though our view of Navy's football program is only from the vantage point of loyal and dedicated fans, the analogies used are relevant to the topic and the story.

No matter the size of your organization or the focus of your business, certain roles are critical to your success, and each of those roles has a few important outcomes that must be targeted. Our hope is that through this book you will find an ally in your quest to target, define, and create methods to produce the outcomes that are vital to your organization. In so doing you can cut through all the noise and be the catalyst for a winning leadership development strategy, one that ignites individual and organization performance so your company can reach new and exciting heights.

Greg Long
Butler Newman

CHAPTER 1

Monday Morning Staff Meeting

THE DOOR TO THE VOLVO WAGON CLOSED WITH A SECURE thud. Aimee Martin glanced over her shoulder to make sure her three-year-old daughter, Kylie, had not left any cherished objects in the backseat. *Whew*, Aimee thought as she eyed the lone remaining Cheerio. *All clear.*

Another smooth drop-off at day care. No complications. She was relieved to realize she would make it to her meeting on time. The squabble she'd had with her husband, Marc, before leaving the house, about why it fell to her to drop Kylie off at day care on the morning of the weekly leadership meeting, had been unfounded after all.

Her office on the east side of Washington, DC, was only twenty minutes away, and traffic flowed smoothly despite the morning drizzle of this early October day. She felt relaxed; her drive was unfolding without a hitch. Aimee, a confident and fit thirty-five-year-old with an impressive track record of success in both her business endeavors and personal life, attacked her commute with the same concentration and efficiency she applied to any other task. She believed in pursuing excellence in all her undertakings.

Aimee felt energized this morning and was looking forward to the Monday morning leadership meeting. That had not always been the case during the four months since her return to Calara Enterprises. The decision to rejoin the workforce had been unexpectedly hard for her. She loved every minute that she spent with Kylie, and it had been hard to imagine anyone else—especially anyone outside the family—caring for her daughter during these formative years. Thankfully, Kylie's transition to day care had surpassed Aimee's best expectations. Kylie loved the social interaction with the staff and the other children and was thriving. Aimee's confidence heading to the office this morning stemmed not from a new sales win but from her peaceful transition from full-time homemaker back to Calara Enterprises.

She wished Calara's sales team was making equal progress with the transition. It was not, however, and Aimee was searching for answers. She had returned to the company specifically to sort through performance issues holding back the sales team. Sales had steadily slipped over the last year, enough so that Calara's competitors were starting to take advantage of that slippage.

Aimee couldn't yet put her finger on the root of the problem. The sales training initiative that had been put in place eighteen months ago had come highly recommended, but it was not well received by the sales force. Staff feedback was that it was too general and not really applicable to the sales role at Calara. The initiative had lost steam over the last few months, and it wasn't immediately obvious how to get sales moving again. This lack of clarity frustrated Aimee. Part of her special talent had always been that solutions for going forward "just came to her" in the midst of whatever chaos existed, but so far, this challenge was different. Calara also seemed different to her. The "our people are important" ethic that she had experienced during her first stint at the company seemed to have eroded.

As Aimee negotiated the steady traffic, her eye caught a screen flash and she heard the chime of her iPhone, resting face up atop her leather-bound journal on the passenger seat. That particular chime indicated a new text message. She glanced over at her phone to check if it was Kylie's day care informing her that she had forgotten after all to send some important item in the rush to get out the door this morning. Instead, she saw Bill's name, her friend and mentor at Calara.

"Bill?" she said aloud to herself. "He never texts me. What could Bill possibly want that warrants a text message? I'll see him in twenty minutes at our meeting!"

She could plainly see the first few words of the message:

> Hi Aimee, sorry to relay this through . . .

She couldn't see the rest without picking up her phone and entering her security code. *Why*, she wondered for the umpteenth time, *did the information technology services group mandate the use of security codes on personal devices?*

She thought about trying to enter the passcode while splitting her attention between the phone keypad and the two cars ahead of her to reveal the rest of Bill's message. Then she remembered how frustrated she gets with other drivers who pull that trick. Even so, she had to fight her curiosity as her right hand instinctively drifted over to her phone. She pulled her hand back to the wheel and her attention back to the road. Bill's message would have to wait.

Aimee's mind went back to the unexpected phone call just over four months ago when Bill had reached out to ask her to consider returning to Calara Enterprises as his "right-hand man" to lead the sales group through a modernization effort. The call had flattered her. Seven years ago he had picked her out of the pack, guiding her through the corporate office maze. She liked him right away, and his counsel had always been sound. Bill had joined Calara within the first year of its formation. He liked to brag that his employee number was 9, still in the single digits. Bill was a smart sales leader, and Calara's founder, Richard, always turned to Bill for advice and guidance on the company's sales strategy and direction. Twenty-four years and much success had cemented Bill's legacy at Calara. Aimee was grateful that during her early years at Calara, Bill had helped her develop a relationship with Richard, who was now retired from the day-to-day operation of the company but stayed engaged as the board chairman.

Since her return, Aimee had noticed the tension between Bill and the new CEO, Ian, who had taken the reins just over a year ago. Although Ian and Bill never disagreed publicly, Aimee could sense the strain in their relationship. She wondered if this strained relationship was behind Bill's odd behavior over the last three weeks. He had grown quiet lately and was not engaging her regarding her efforts to reverse the sales team's slump.

Almost before the car fully stopped, Aimee threw the car in park and switched off the ignition in one fluid motion. She left her door closed, however, as she picked up her phone and impatiently typed in her passcode to retrieve Bill's text:

> Hi Aimee, sorry to relay this through a text message. I wanted to give you a heads-up that I've made a sudden decision to change course. Can't explain. You'll do great.
>
> Bill

Aimee read the message again—first quickly, then slowly, picking apart each word. *This can't be good*, she thought as she sat frozen behind the wheel. Air rushed from her lungs, just like when Kylie had accidently kicked her in the stomach last week.

Still staring at the message and only half aware of what she was doing, Aimee slid her thumb across the screen to locate Bill's number and hit Call Mobile. With each ring Aimee grew more anxious.

"You've reached Bill McCray. Leave a brief message and I will return your call as soon as I am able." It was the sound of Bill's voice-mail message. Now Aimee felt like kicking herself, thinking she should have called him back as soon as she got the text. "Doggone it!" she said to no one.

Aimee gathered her belongings quickly and headed to the eight-story building bearing the Calara logo. *Maybe I can catch Bill on the way to the conference room before the meeting starts*, she thought as she headed across the parking lot.

⋮

There was no sign of Bill in the hallway, so Aimee stepped into the conference room. She quickly scanned the polished mahogany table as everyone gathered for the leadership meeting. The three empty seats near the head of the table confirmed Bill's absence, but Ian and the new marketing guy, Conroy, were also missing from the gathering. *Maybe I'm overreacting*, Aimee thought, reflecting back on Bill's text.

As she worked her way around the large table to her usual seat, she was greeted in typical fashion by Faith, her longtime colleague and the CFO.

"Hi, Aimee. How was your weekend?" Faith asked pleasantly.

"Not bad. Not bad." Aimee responded on autopilot, distracted by the fact that the chair beside her, usually occupied by Bill, remained empty.

She landed in her seat with an unenthusiastic thud that was atypical of her energetic style, and she felt a little uncomfortable that Faith had noticed. She took a deep breath and surveyed the room again. The air was filled with the normal Monday morning buzz—stories of weekend victories and laments at how fast the year was flying by. No one was acting the least bit out of the ordinary. Surely she was reading too much into the cryptic note Bill had sent to her.

Aimee exhaled a deep sigh and began readying her mind for the meeting in front of her. It had taken a few months for her to get used to the hurried cadence that had become typical of the beginning of each week since she had returned.

Conroy entered the room first, only a step ahead of Ian and both shot to two of the open seats near the head of the table. Conroy's face betrayed such a smug air of satisfaction, it looked as if all his favorite college football teams had won their weekend gridiron matches handily. Victory was written all over his face, and he visibly worked to constrain his joy.

Aimee's stomach immediately tightened at the sight. Ian had brought Conroy on board about two months before Aimee's return, and though she did not know him well, she had been suspicious of him from the start. From Aimee's vantage point, Conroy had shown no interest in collaborating with either Bill or her as he worked to formulate the new marketing strategy for Calara. He seemed always in a hurry and did little to understand the perspective of the people who had built Calara. Clearly Conroy was convinced he had a better way.

Aimee didn't agree. Their big difference was in their perspective of the frontline sales reps. Conroy believed in a top-down approach. Those from corporate, usually Conroy and others like him, would decide the answer and tell everyone exactly what to do—what tactics to follow, what accounts to focus on, and so on. The sales reps' job was simply to execute the program or follow up the marketing campaign.

By contrast, Aimee inherently looked to the people on the front line. Experience had shown her that they were closest to the action, and that gave them a strong and relevant perspective that could inform executive decisions. Where she struggled, however, was how to capture and boil down that frontline perspective in a way that was straightforward to understand and apply.

"Well, let's get started," Ian said as he settled into his seat. The weekend buzz quickly abated and the group turned its attention to Ian. Bill's chair remained empty.

"I'd like to begin with an update on the marketing front. Conroy?" Ian continued as he nodded in Conroy's direction.

Conroy smiled broadly, but before he could get the first word out of his mouth, Aimee interrupted.

"Ian, don't you think we should wait another minute for Bill? I know he will be interested in the latest on the marketing front."

"No, we can begin," Ian said curtly. "Conroy?"

"Thanks, Ian." Conroy stood up, which was not customary for this meeting. He had just been handed the stage, and clearly he was going to take maximum advantage of it.

"Well, as I mentioned briefly a couple of weeks ago, I've been working on a plan to radically change the way we go to market. This plan will springboard Calara Enterprises into the modern—into the digital age," he said with a smirk, "even if it is kicking and screaming."

As the rest of her colleagues gave a polite chuckle, Aimee dropped her head and stared at the blank page in her journal lying open on the table in front of her. The overbearing manner in which Conroy was delivering his message created knots in her stomach.

"Ian and I worked much of the weekend to finalize the framework of the plan, and we're both very excited to brief you on it—"

Aimee suddenly brought her head back upright and swung her chair to face Ian. "Ian, have you gotten Bill's input on this plan?" she interrupted Conroy without apology.

Conroy shifted and positioned himself to continue his briefing, acting as if neither he nor anyone else in the room had heard Aimee's fiery reaction.

"Wait, Conroy." Ian held up a hand, reasserting control over the meeting. "Let me address Aimee's concern."

He turned to face her. "Aimee, that's a valid question. However, you all should know that, despite my best efforts to persuade him otherwise, Bill has resigned—effective immediately."

A hush filled the room. Conroy remained standing, facing the rest of the team, clearly the only one in the room who was not surprised at the news. He tried to feign a sad look but fooled no one.

As Ian continued, Aimee could feel the eyes of the leadership team as they stole glances at her, curious at her reaction. The color drained from her face as she glared in Ian's direction. A hundred thoughts raced through her mind. She felt alone without her ally and mentor, isolated at the table among the other leaders of Calara.

Ian continued, "I know that you would like to hear more in this regard; however, Bill and I both agreed not to share the details of our discussions—beyond the final result, that is. So while I know that this news is disruptive, I urge us all to stay focused on our task at hand. I will be working with each of you in the days ahead to understand the impact of this change and what we must do to push forward.

"Conroy, please continue with your briefing," Ian said quietly but firmly.

Aimee didn't hear another word Conroy had to say. She felt betrayed on all fronts. Betrayed by Bill, who hadn't given her any indication of what he must have known was coming. Betrayed by Ian. None of this made sense. Why had Bill hired her to help him move the company forward and modernize sales if he was planning to go soon? For all intents and purposes, Bill had vanished and left her to face the challenges alone.

⋮

Aimee closed the door behind her as she returned to her office. *What is going on?* She wanted to just leave, pick up Kylie, and call it a day. She quickly pushed those thoughts aside. She knew leaving early would be seen as a sign of weakness by Conroy, and she wouldn't give him the satisfaction.

Her thoughts wandered back to her earliest days with the company. She drew strength from the memories of a different Calara. It had been an electric time. Everyone was engaged in moving the mission forward, extending the growth streak, and ultimately taking the company public. The work hadn't always gone perfectly, but there were never any crazy surprises like today's.

She smiled as she remembered how she was initially afraid of Bill. His intensity intimidated her, but before long, she adjusted to his style and the two of them clicked. The more she understood him, the more Bill came to rely on her. She also had built a strong relationship with Joe, one of their early sales rep hires. He shook things up by consistently blowing his numbers out of the water. Bill and Aimee never completely understood just how he worked his magic. But whatever his secret was, the three of them together became an unstoppable force, consistently performing above expectations. They even played together as a team: Bill introduced Aimee and Joe to his passion for the sport of cycling, and they often took early morning rides together before the office opened.

That alchemy between sales and management to produce results was just what she and Bill had been trying to revive among the sales force. Now with Bill gone, she was sorry that she hadn't spent more time with Joe upon her return. If nothing else came from today, at least she would commit to spend more time with Joe and get his perspective on how to reinvigorate Calara and return it to the productivity of old.

Before she even quite realized what she was doing, she reached for her office phone and dialed Bill's number on impulse. He must be able to tell her something about what was going on— he owed her that much.

The phone didn't even ring before voice mail picked up: "I'm sorry to have missed your call. . . ."

Aimee sighed. But no sooner had she hung up the receiver than the soft ring of her desk phone was announcing another call.

"Good morning, this is Aimee," she said brightly, expecting to hear the sound of her former mentor's voice on the other end. Instead, she immediately started scowling as the customer on the other end of the line unloaded a tirade of complaints. While listening, Aimee picked up her sales territory sheet and saw that this was one of former sale rep Frank's customers. She'd been worried something like this might happen when Frank suddenly quit.

"That's correct, Frank is no longer with us. No, I can't discuss the reasons for his departure. Yes, it was sudden. No, I'm not aware of your situation, but if you'll take a minute to explain." Immediately Aimee was almost sorry she asked, but still she listened intently.

"My deepest apologies, Mr. Cameron. I can tell that you're upset, and I'd like to meet with you face to face to better understand the situation and determine how best to rectify it." Aimee seamlessly shifted into customer repair mode, shrugging off the shock and disappointments of what transpired in the morning leadership meeting. Her ability to change gears quickly was one of her strengths as a manager.

"Yes, I agree. You have every right to be upset. That is not how we operate. You have my commitment that I will personally sort this out and get it fixed." Aimee's directness and comforting tone were having the desired effect.

"How about your office at nine a.m. tomorrow morning?… Again, please accept my apologies. Obviously this should have been attended to much sooner. I will call you when I arrive in your lobby. Thanks, Mr. Cameron, for letting me know. Yes, you can be confident we will make this right."

The phone was still rocking in its cradle when Aimee swung open her door and bolted down the hall to her administrative assistant's desk.

"Doris, find Joe and clear both our schedules for tomorrow. Tell him I need him to go with me to Richmond this afternoon. We'll leave at three for a critical customer meeting. Tell him I'll brief him in the car."

In a military-like about-face, Aimee headed back to her office to call Marc to arrange for Kylie's pickup at day care, while still barking orders to Doris over her shoulder. "And pull all of PBH's and Frank's other customer files. I need them on my desk as soon as possible."

She set her jaw determinedly. There would be no more surprises around Calara—not if she could help it.

CHAPTER 2

Ride from Richmond

"Thanks again for coming with me on such short notice, Joe," Aimee said as he slid into the Volvo's passenger side, ready for the ride back to the office.

"Sure, no problem," Joe replied with a sure and confident smile.

At age fifty-one, Joe had a fit form that was a testament to his passion for cycling, but his staid manner of dress belied his years in the sales business. A simple button-down shirt, khaki slacks, and a blue blazer were his standard wardrobe. No fancy suits for Joe, even though, based on his sales track record, he could easily afford them. He had a knack for getting close to his customers in an authentic way that led to deep, lasting, and very profitable relationships. His uncanny relationship skills supported Joe comfortably and allowed him to send his daughter to Georgetown and his son to Notre Dame. Joe had spent his entire adult life in sales of one type or another but really seemed to settle in at Calara Enterprises.

"I don't know what I would have done in there without you," Aimee continued. Joe smiled and gazed out the window at the passing scenery, as if receiving so much heartfelt praise made this modest man just a tad uncomfortable.

"I reviewed all of Frank's files yesterday. I don't think this is the only customer of his that has potential problems. How did we miss this? I guess I've been focused too much on internal matters lately." Aimee was talking to herself as much as to Joe.

He had turned his head back to face her and nodded as she spoke.

"We need to reassign all of his accounts. And we need someone experienced to take over the PBH account. That one is really important to us." Aimee mentally ran through the list of reps in this region and came up empty. She paused, hoping for Joe to offer up a name.

He didn't.

She glanced at him. "Okay, so we don't have someone proven, someone with the right level of experience. Looks like we'll need to hire someone, but who?"

Joe smiled. "It will take too long to hire someone from outside and get them up to speed in time to have any impact on the PBH account. But I do have an idea. It's a little risky, however."

Aimee frowned. "What or whom do you have in mind?"

"Sally," Joe offered.

Aimee had met Sally briefly at a regional sales meeting. She seemed personable and carried herself well. But she was so green. She had been with the company for only six months. *We do so little to prepare new reps at Calara these days,* Aimee thought as she processed Joe's idea.

"Sally? I don't know." Aimee unconsciously shook her head from side to side. "I don't think she has the right level of experience."

Aimee was frustrated. If only she could just hire a superstar, plug that person in on the PBH account, and not have to worry about it further. Though she hesitated to admit it, she knew that wouldn't work. Everyone in the industry wanted to hire people from the limited supply of truly top talent. Calara had its fair share of top performers like Joe, but she wanted more. She sighed because she knew it was unrealistic to simply hire them. What she really needed was a way to help good people achieve sales success at Calara. But how? How do you get great results from good people?

She said, "I guess Sally could be a possibility, but you know as well as I do that we're not out of the woods yet with PBH. Is she up to this kind of challenge? Even I'm not clear how we should handle this customer and turn the account around. I'm especially disappointed that Frank let the account deteriorate so badly. I anticipated PBH growing into a big account—and having real impact on our fourth quarter."

"Not to worry, Aimee. Mr. Cameron is going to come around. We'll be fine. Sally will do a great job, and I'll back her up all the way. We won't let you down."

"How can you be so sure, Joe?"

"I have dealt with clients like this a dozen times before—with a dozen different names in a dozen different companies. Mr. Cameron is just looking for someone he can trust. This was his first test to see if we can be that kind of partner."

Joe's confidence was like that of a pro golfer who had just hit a spectacular approach shot on his home course. His statement hung in the air for a moment just like a small white golf ball bouncing in the middle of a deep-green fairway.

Aimee's gut instinct told her Joe would see this through. *I just need a way to clone Joe,* she mused. *That's what I need to figure out. How do I make more Joes?* She realized that was the problem at Calara—the success of sales reps had been left up to chance or, worse yet, to "wishful" hiring.

Just then, the distinctive ring of an incoming call through the Volvo's Bluetooth phone connection interrupted her thoughts.

Conroy's name displayed on the console screen in the center of the dashboard. *Oh great—Conroy. I really don't want to talk to him right now.* But she reached out and pressed the Accept button on the console anyway.

"Hello?"

"Aimee, it's Conroy."

"Yes, Conroy, what's up?"

"You missed the webinar this morning on digital selling." His barbed tone was even sharper than normal. "It was important for you to be there. At last week's leadership meeting we all committed to attend, *remember*?" His sarcasm made it not so much a question as an accusation.

"Ian really noticed your absence," he continued, "so I told him I'd give you a call to follow up. This doesn't have anything to do with Bill, does it?"

"No, Conroy. Nothing like that." Aimee was short in her retort and then fell silent, not trusting herself to control her anger with Conroy.

"Hello, Aimee, are you still there? Did we lose the connection? Aimee?" Conroy blasted, irritation building with each word.

"Yep, still here," Aimee returned in an even tone that betrayed nothing.

"Aimee, do you have any idea, *any idea*, the trouble I went through to line up ACP for a private presentation of this webinar?" Conroy's rage was building and totally disproportionate to the circumstance.

"Conroy," Aimee replied, her even tone recalling the times she cooled Kylie down from a temper tantrum, "I know you like this expert from ACP, and from the little research I've done, he seems pretty credible. But come on, don't make this into such a big deal—"

"Aimee, this *is* a big deal!"

"Please slow down, Conroy. Let's talk about this." Aimee tried once again to restore some calm to the conversation.

There was no reply.

"Conroy…Conroy, are you there?"

The familiar sound of a disconnected line abruptly emanated from the speaker.

She glanced at the dashboard control screen, expecting to see the message "Call failed." Instead, she saw the routine message "Call ended."

"He hung up on me." Aimee said, incredulous.

"What?" Joe, who had obviously been listening to the conversation, chimed in.

"Oh, nothing," Aimee said quickly. "We must have lost our connection."

"Come on, Aimee, what gives? I couldn't help but overhear Conroy and his tone."

"It's nothing…I think. Don't worry about it."

Aimee wanted to open up to Joe and let him in on what was behind Bill's abrupt departure, but she couldn't. Not yet. She needed to know more about what was going on with Conroy and the digital selling initiative with ACP. The last thing she needed was to unnecessarily spook Joe and undermine his productivity. Until she had a firm grasp on what was going on and how to move forward, she would insulate Joe from the craziness.

"Conroy was upset that I missed a meeting this morning that he had planned for over a week. I'm sure Doris told him I couldn't attend when she cleared our calendars for today."

"Maybe he just missed the message," Joe offered. "But did he ask you where you were instead of the meeting?"

"No. The thought that I might have a more pressing issue than his meeting apparently never crossed his mind." Aimee had meant for that reply to sound offhand, but she could hear the frustration in her voice and knew Joe heard it, too.

Joe nodded and then looked out the window thoughtfully.

"We are where we needed to be today, Joe—with a key customer. I just hope this Mr. Cameron comes through for us. I'm counting on you to guide Sally. We can't drop the ball again."

"I'll guide Sally to make sure Mr. Cameron comes around," Joe reassured her, relaxing as the conversation turned back to more comfortable ground. "I guarantee it."

⋮

After she dropped Joe off at the office, Aimee stayed in the parking lot and placed a call to Faith. She wanted to get Faith's read on the situation with Conroy. Aimee had always been able to rely on Faith's guidance to help her navigate the politics of Calara.

"Hello, Faith, it's Aimee. Thanks for picking up so late."

"Sure, what's up?" Faith's question carried no surprise.

"Hey, I just needed a sounding board. I think I screwed up with Conroy and have gotten myself into hot water. Did Conroy say anything to you?"

"Yes, he called and was pretty upset. I tried to talk him down a bit. I said that I was sure you had a good reason for missing the meeting."

"That's just it, Faith. He didn't even ask where I was or what had pulled me away."

"So where were you?"

"I was with Joe making an emergency call on a client. Frank really bungled this one," she explained. "I think we managed to avert the worst, at least for the time being. Joe was really good, as always. We'll get the relationship back in order."

"I suspected it was something like that. I know we can always count on you to handle the tough situations with clients. That is one of the reasons we brought you back."

"Thanks, Faith. But what about Conroy?" Aimee's confidence waned as she shifted the conversation.

"Conroy's upset, very upset," Faith's tone was sharp. "The digital strategy initiative is important."

"Of course," Aimee demurred, a bit surprised by Faith's tone. "I'll call him tomorrow. Any advice on how to approach the conversation to get past this?"

Faith's pause was longer than expected and much longer than was typical in a conversation with Aimee. The dead silence caused Aimee's stomach to do a flip.

"Okay, I won't call. I'll go to his office to meet him—"

"Meanwhile," Faith cut Aimee short—her voice had transformed from that of a reassuring confidant to that of a person in a position of authority—"you need to know I've asked Doris to put some time on the calendar for us tomorrow to talk about the quarter's projections. We have to make sure we're meeting the street's expectations. There are some hard choices ahead for us all."

"I see" was the only response that Aimee could muster. "I'll see you tomorrow."

"I'll see you tomorrow," Faith concluded abruptly.

Aimee felt sick. She didn't need to know the details to understand that tomorrow's conversation would be an unpleasant one.

CHAPTER 3

Changing Faith

FAITH'S OFFICE HAD ALWAYS SEEMED WARM AND FULL OF cheer. Maybe it was the fact that the overcast day blocked any hint of sunshine or the tone in Faith's voice last night was coloring Aimee's perceptions in a new way—whatever it was, Aimee twitched in the chair, her arms folded to ward off the chill she was experiencing as she waited for Faith to return from the printer. Aimee wasn't used to feeling this way when it came to Faith. The two of them had always maintained an open and supportive relationship. The warmth, even in Faith's greeting as Aimee came into her office, was absent. It occurred to Aimee that this was symbolic of the new Calara itself.

Faith held the unstapled sheets of paper close to her body as she returned to the office. Without a word, she found her way around her large, well-managed desk and placed the freshly printed pages face down in front of her. Aimee waited silently, arms still folded, for Faith to speak. Her nature was to jump right in and break the silence, but she resisted. This was Faith's meeting: *I'll wait for her to set the tone*, Aimee reasoned. Besides, even if their communication styles were different, in the end they all wanted the same thing—business results. Since they were aligned on that, surely they would eventually align on how to go about it.

"Aimee, I really…we all really appreciate the way you have jumped in to keep things going since Bill's departure. Yesterday's Richmond trip is just one example."

"Thanks."

"One of the tasks that Conroy was helping Bill with was a review of our overhead associated with the sales force." Faith picked up the papers from the desk—keeping them close as she found the right words for Aimee. "Changes are going on that require us all to think differently about the way sales operates."

What changes? Aimee realized Conroy had lots of ideas about how to change the marketing approach, but what sales changes has he convinced Faith of? *What*, she wondered, *could Conroy possibly know about the sales force?*

"Conroy finished his analysis late yesterday. Bottom line: we need to reduce our sales force substantially, with a 20 percent cut immediately."

The clipped cadence of Faith's words did not invite comment from Aimee as Faith diverted her eyes from Aimee's face and busied herself with the papers on her desk.

Though Aimee did not speak, every fiber of her body was sounding an alarm. She knew from the phone call yesterday that this was not going to be a pleasant meeting, but this was worse than she thought. Canning the very people who held the relationship with the customers? This was a short-term fix to reduce costs that would jeopardize the long-term profitability of the company. What was Faith thinking?

"Aimee, there are tough choices to make. Here is the recommended list of initial cuts that Conroy developed based on an analysis of last quarter's sales results."

The two women avoided eye contact as Faith pushed the list across the desk to Aimee, who reluctantly received it. Without glancing up, Aimee began to scan the list. As she did, she realized the names were mostly people that had joined the company during her absence. Then her eyes landed on a familiar name.

"What? Faith, you've got to be kidding!" Aimee blurted. "Joe Fabri is on this list! There is no way he should be remotely considered. Conroy is nuts!"

The sudden anger in her voice broke the tension in the room in a way that caught Faith off guard. Aimee sprang to her feet, towering over Faith, who remained impassive behind her desk.

"Faith, what is going on?" Aimee's internal alarms started going off. "Why is Joe on this list? Why is there even a list?"

"Aimee, you know that we've been under serious market pressures over the last few months," Faith replied frostily. "One of the reasons Conroy had the lead in developing the list is that we wanted to take the emotional element out of the process." Faith eyed Aimee as if to underscore her point. "Joe's numbers must not have been good enough last quarter when compared to his cost to the company," she concluded dismissively.

Aimee had no doubt in her mind that Faith and Conroy were approaching this all wrong, with potentially disastrous results. She knew there was a better way to solve this challenge, but she just couldn't quite articulate it.

The best she could come up with at the moment was "Is this final? Will Conroy be taking action on all of these people—will he look them in the eye to give them the news?"

Faith folded her arms across her chest; she was in full authoritative mode. "No, taking action on the list is totally your responsibility. We would like this to be wrapped up by the end of the month. Let me know your plan as soon as possible."

Faith returned her gaze to the papers on the desk as she added, "And as always, don't hesitate to call me with questions."

Aimee took her cue. Without speaking another word, she folded the list in half, turned, and left. *Faith has lost touch with the people who make the company go*, Aimee thought. One of the reasons they had become such close colleagues over the years was Faith's empathy for the people on the front line, those who did the hard work every day to keep the company moving and, until recently, growing. Whatever was behind her change of attitude didn't matter. This was not the same Faith that she had come to know and trust.

⋮

Aimee gritted her teeth for the rest of the day and reluctantly plodded through the remaining meetings on her calendar. When she finally returned to her office, she bypassed the motion detector on the wall light switch. Her head pounded with a relentless and sharp pain just in back of both eyes, and she didn't want to face the bright, artificial glare of the overhead fluorescent lights.

Aimee sat alone in her office in the near dark. The day was lost. She did not remember a single conversation since she had left Faith's office. The list Faith had given her remained folded in half and tucked into her journal, which lay open in front of her. Although emotionally she was dreading it, her business mind was telling her to pull out the list and review it in detail. She needed to start formulating her plan regarding each of the individuals on the page.

As she grasped the folded paper, she stopped short of pulling the page out and looking at it again. She knew who was on the list. Joe was on the list. This was all that mattered. Her heart sank. This was no longer the Calara that she—and Bill and Joe, for that matter—had helped to build.

As much as she admired Bill over the course of her career, at this moment she resented him. How could he leave her with this mess? He had to have known what was going on. Did he just bail? Maybe that explains why he didn't talk with her before he left. Maybe he was feeling guilty for leaving her with all the hard decisions. She still couldn't get over his leaving without warning. If he were still here, Aimee knew she would be sitting in Bill's office right now talking this over with him, and together they would sort out the whole mess.

She could hear Bill's voice in her head. "Aimee, you know what your problem is. You don't want to fire Joe because you admire him—you want to be like him. In many respects you are just like him, just a younger, more up-to-date version. You and Joe and I, we're all alike. We care that our customers' needs are met. When we have a conversation with any one of our customers, we are having a conversation with a person, a person who needs our help to succeed. We know this is not only the right way to be, it's the smart way to be."

Aimee knew this notion was absolutely right. She chuckled to herself. *Bill's not even here and he's still giving me advice.*

A flood of emotion hit her. Calara has been built into a successful company on strong connections with its customers—connections that come not through a slick digital marketing message but through dedicated efforts of people like Joe and her. She couldn't even imagine Conroy in front of a customer. She tried to picture Conroy, armed with his defensive remarks and condescending attitude, conducting the meeting with Mr. Cameron in Richmond instead of using the can-do, we'll-make-it-right approach taken by Joe and her. *What a disaster!* she thought.

Aimee pulled the list from her journal and turned on the lights. As she stood over her desk reading the list, really reading it for the first time, the truth of the situation struck her squarely: if Joe goes, the stage is set for everyone like Joe to go. Joe is the first domino in a long line of sales team dominos—that would end with her.

She felt the blood drain from her face. *This can't be happening.*

Beyond her own situation, Aimee could see that without the skill of the sales team and the relationships it had forged with clients, Calara Enterprises' position in the marketplace would be in danger.

Her thoughts turned back to Bill. *Where is he?* Though she had always strived to be like Bill, it suddenly struck her that in this important matter she would not be like Bill and just abandon ship. She could not turn her back on Joe. She had to come up with a game plan.

Her mind now racing, searching frantically for a solution, she returned to her stiff office chair.

Bill may not want to be found. The reality hit her. Her body stiffened to match the chair, but her mind was flooded with conflicted thoughts, subconsciously scanning every avenue for a possible path out of this mess. She kept thinking about Calara's business and her history with the company. Aimee grabbed her journal and began to doodle on the first blank page.

She wrote the word "People" at the top of the page. She intuitively knew that the ultimate answer lay with the people, the sales

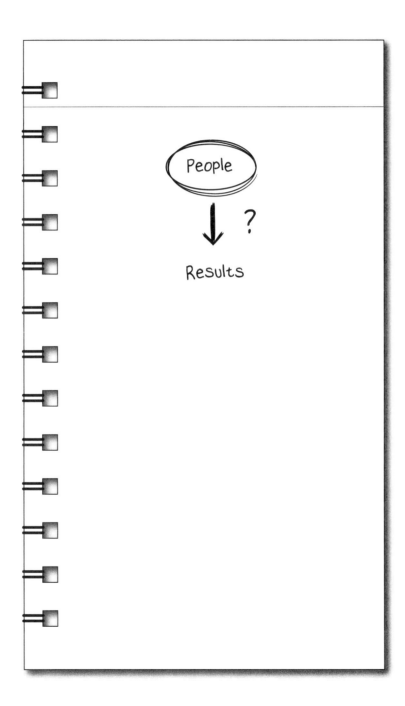

force, who had daily contact with their customers. A bit further down the page she added the word "Results." Without question, that was what they were ultimately after.

Aimee's spirit brightened as she rapidly drew several circles around "People" and then added an arrow down the page from "People" to "Results." She reinforced the arrow to make it stand out even more. *How do I tie these together?* Aimee thought as she added a question mark next to her arrow. Take the new sales rep, Sally: how do we help new people like Sally gain clarity about the job we are asking them to do so they know not only what targets to hit but how to hit them?

Aimee scrutinized the page in front of her and almost through reflex added the word "Good" in front of "People" and "Great" in front of "Results." This was the question that haunted her: "How do we help good people achieve great results?"

Her doodling slowed and seemed to lose focus as she pondered this question. Then, out of nowhere, another name popped up: Shafe, her older brother. A football coach and former player himself, Shafe had a different way of looking at situations and had always offered her good advice over the years.

Her pulse picked up and the color returned to her face. *He'll give me a fresh perspective.* She figured she could catch him between team practice sessions if she called him on the way into the office tomorrow. She smiled as she glanced down at her doodles again. People, yes. And the person to count on now was Shafe.

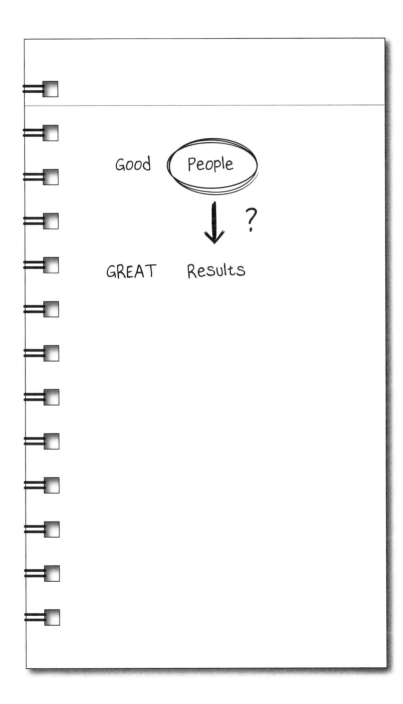

CHAPTER 4

Coach Shafe

As Aimee settled in for her westward journey on Route 50 to her office just outside of DC, the sign for Rowe Boulevard, the exit that led to the Naval Academy, reminded her of conversations with her brother. Shafe lived and breathed football. He started playing in Pee Wees when he was six and fell more in love with the sport every year. She loved her big brother. She also loved the fact that all her female friends refer to him as "Clark Kent" on account of his jet-black hair, chiseled jaw, and broad shoulders atop his six foot, four inch frame.

When Shafe got the job as the offensive line coach at the Naval Academy, he was so excited it was hard to put up with him. Every conversation turned to football. Before long, Aimee felt as if she could coach the offensive line alongside Shafe. She had listened to so many impassioned explanations of football offenses, blocking schemes, and audibles or audios or whatever they called that stuff. But, she had to admit, Shafe's passion for the game drove him and those around him to new heights. Navy actually had a pretty good football team, and Shafe's passion was no doubt part of Navy's success using the triple-option offense. Shafe spoke of the triple option admiringly—a multifaceted offense that relies mostly on running plays. Maybe, thought Aimee, she could translate some of that passion into something usable for Calara's sales team.

She strained to recall what Shafe had tried to explain to her over Thanksgiving dinner last year. He told her the key to Navy's wins was somehow connected to scoring and time of possession of the ball.

"Oh gee, brother, winning has to do with scoring? Duh!" she'd teased him then. "Pass the turkey, will you?"

Now she wished she had actually paid attention. Had he been talking about how long it took to score or how to score with possession of the ball? And what about passion for playing the game? How did that factor in?

She reflected back on the situation with Mr. Cameron in Richmond. Lots of people had a passion for growing the business. But not all of them could channel that into action that mattered. Aimee knew she could always count on Joe, who consistently managed to convert his passion into tangible results on the front line of sales. But what she didn't know was his secret for doing it. Did he understand something that no one else did? Did he just care more? Or did he think about sales from a different perspective? Whatever it was, he was clearly more effective than most. Somehow, Aimee felt Shafe held clues that would help her get a new perspective on her sales team and fix the problems that lay ahead.

She pushed the Voice command button on the steering wheel, said "Call Shafe on mobile," and waited for the computer voice to respond: "Calling Shafe on mobile."

"Hey, Sis," he answered quickly.

"Hi, Shafe." Second thoughts gripped Aimee. Maybe she shouldn't bother him with her work woes. Shafe was in the middle of football season and must be overloaded already.

"Sis?"

"I know you're busy…maybe I should call back."

"What's wrong?"

"I really don't want to bother you."

"Talk to me, Aimee."

Aimee smiled—Shafe, always in problem-solving mode. "It's just work," she replied. "It seems to keep getting worse, and now they want me to fire one of my top sales reps before the end of the month! I feel in some weird way like it's an attack on me, too. Not only that, this is all going to end up compromising Calara's success."

"Okay. Okay. Let's back up. Do you really think that the company would allow something like that to happen? Why are they saying that your rep's going to be let go?"

"Profits this quarter are down. They are looking for ways to quickly cut costs." Aimee paused. "What they are forgetting is that Joe is one of our top performers. If I had lots more reps like Joe, more performing at his level, our sales team would drive the business through this slump."

"Tell me how I can help, Sis."

"That's just it, Shafe. I can't stop thinking about your passion around getting your linemen to perform. How do you get such consistent performance? Can I use the same principles here for our sales team?"

"Well, that's an interesting thought. I've never really considered how our approach might be used in a business environment. What led you to this connection?"

"I don't know, Shafe. Partly it's you. You might not realize it, but I really hear the way you talk about your guys—how they are always giving their all. How the line is key to Navy's turnaround." Aimee paused. "I know it's a stretch, but performance is performance, right? There has to be something in your approach that I can use."

"There you go again, Sis. Always thinking out of the box and looking for clarity. I love that about you. You could be on to something here. What's the one thing that you and your sales team focus on?"

"Sales or revenue, I suppose."

"Okay, that makes sense, but you have to get more specific."

"What do you mean? What's more specific than revenue?" Aimee asked with a renewed interest. She had always taken for granted that revenue was the end goal, the thing they should all focus on. But Shafe's question immediately sparked an entirely new train of thought. What if she hadn't thought deeply enough yet about the end goal?

Shafe continued, "Look. I'm slammed right now, but can you stop by one day after practice? We can start to map out some potential ways that Navy's approach to equipping the team on the football field may help you with your sales team."

"Shafe, that would be great!" Aimee told him—and then hesitated. "You're not just being nice, are you? The idea doesn't sound too far-fetched?"

"Absolutely not! Keep your chin up, Sis. I predict a game-winning score in your future. Whatever you do, don't let the nonsense get you down."

"Thanks, Shafe. See you soon." Aimee pushed the End Call button on the console as she gave an audible sigh of relief.

⋮

Aimee whistled her own rendition of the Navy fight song as she walked quickly past the BMW, Audi, and Infiniti in the employee parking garage. She had a spring in her step that had been absent since Faith gave her Conroy's plan for eliminating jobs. She could hardly wait until her visit with Shafe next week. She was sure she was on to something—something that would not only transform the sales group but could spread to other places within the company. As she waved her security badge past the door reader, she reached into her small purse and grabbed her iPhone to quickly confirm her schedule. As usual, she was among the first in the building and she had an hour before her first meeting. Without thinking, she pushed the up arrow by the elevator door.

Aimee mentally began to map out questions she had to ask Shafe. How does he pick the starting lineup? How does he equip not only the starting players but the backups with what they need to get such consistent performance across the board, especially given the recruiting challenges Navy faces. Highly sought-after recruits from linemen to quarterbacks always shy away from Navy as a choice. The best high school players have pro football careers as their aspiration, and a five-year commitment to serve in the military makes a pro football career next to impossible. So who comes to Navy to play football? And what strategy do her brother and the rest of the coaching staff use to ensure they are competitive against other teams? How do they get such great results out of players who otherwise aren't superstars? What makes the difference? So many questions!

"I know! Joe!" Aimee said out loud, standing alone in the middle of the quiet morning elevator. It was all coming together: Joe loves football. He is always spouting off sports analogies. She'd talk through her questions with him before her meeting with her brother.

Joe was always her go-to guy. For new ideas, difficult customers, training for new reps—whatever she needed, Joe always came through. That's why she knew she had to put a stop to the nonsense about firing Joe. She admitted his sales had been a little down over the last quarter, but he was experimenting with the positioning of the new product suite. Joe was the first to notice that the old messaging was not going to work, and he was at the forefront of working out a new value proposition. *No way we'll let him go.*

She quickly shifted back to thinking about the sales team. *The Calara Offensive Sales Strategy, modeled after the famed Navy Triple Option. Joe is going to love it!*

The elevator door completed its lazy opening sequence, and Aimee quickly stepped out, her heels clicking down the nicely decorated hallway to her windowed office overlooking the atrium. As she rounded the corner, Aimee suddenly stopped and cocked her head slightly. What were those noises? As she listened closer, it sounded like Ian and Faith talking. Their voices were coming from her office—and her office light was on. What was happening?

Aimee's heartbeat quickened as with each step she confirmed the curious gathering in *her* office, her island of sanity in this otherwise crazy existence.

"Hi, Ian. Hi, Faith." Aimee summoned a firm tone as she crossed the threshold. The comfortable banter that Aimee had detected earlier from the hallway evaporated. "Didn't expect to find you two here. What's going on—am I about to get fired?" Aimee asked in an offhand, joking tone that belied the nervousness she felt.

Ian was first to speak. "No, no, of course not, Aimee."

Faith chimed in: "Please, sit down. We apologize if we startled you. We all have a packed day ahead of us and Ian and I wanted to give you a quick heads-up."

"Heads-up? Heads-up about what?" Aimee's voice was missing its usual upbeat tone.

"Don't get concerned—it's good news. Things are moving fast around here right now. Lots of new ideas and the need to stir things up." Ian paused to gauge Aimee's reaction.

Ian looked surprised when Aimee smiled slightly as she suddenly saw the unplanned meeting as an opportunity to change Ian's and Faith's minds regarding cutting the sales force.

"I know that Faith has talked to you about the need to downsize the sales organization. We're not taking such action lightly. We both want you to realize that," Ian continued.

"I do realize it, and that's why I want to talk it through. This is a major change in direction, and we all need to understand the implications to our customers."

Ian cut her off. "Believe me, Aimee, we've already been through this. We weighed the pros and cons and have settled on a course."

Ian's tone shattered Aimee's hope of guiding the conversation to an about-face on the downsizing. Instead she suddenly found herself defensively reacting to Ian.

"So does that mean the decision is final? How can you make such a decision without a lot more discussion?" Aimee's voice clearly showed signs of frustration.

"Nothing's final, Aimee," Faith jumped in. "Look, I'll book some time for you and me to begin to map out our direction in regard to the sales function."

The room had become uncomfortable. Aimee looked out the window and away from the two intruders to gather her composure. She wouldn't let them get the best of her in this "friendly" ambush.

Faith continued, "Actually, we didn't come here to talk about the sales organization."

"Really? What then?" To Aimee's mind, nothing was more important than saving the sales team.

"We just wanted to give you a heads-up that Conroy will be stopping by later today. He's going to ask for your help on the new initiative that he's spearheading," Ian said. His reversion to his usual matter-of-fact style calmed Aimee somewhat. "Conroy is onto something, Aimee. I think it will move the company to the next level."

"Conroy's new project will go a lot better with your help and support, Aimee," said Faith. Her tone shifted abruptly to that of mentor and confidant. "Just hear Conroy out when he stops by. That's all we ask."

"The company needs you to be on board, Aimee," Ian concluded as he quickly stood and moved toward the door.

"Let's talk again after you and Conroy have connected," Faith said in a reassuring tone as she followed Ian out of Aimee's office.

As soon as she heard the elevator door close and the muffled tones of Ian and Faith disappear, Aimee jumped up and slammed her door. The forceful bang would have garnered attention up and down the hallway had anyone else been on the floor at this hour.

Aimee stood motionless. Her shoulders arched against the sturdy oak, unconsciously bracing the door shut lest any additional intruders attempt to violate the sanctuary that she meticulously maintained.

What had this place become? Aimee was disappointed in Faith—using their friendship to manipulate her to support some cockamamie plan of Conroy's. Aimee never wanted to open her office door again. She sighed. What made her think she could just walk back into the work world and pick up where she had left off? She had initially been so optimistic, comforted by the numerous successes she had achieved before she took time off to start her family. But the whole place was different now. Decisions were made in late-night private sessions instead of in team meetings and discussions. There were factions and alliances and secrets. What a mess! The old openness and team spirit seemed to be gone. Also gone was the willingness to think outside the box—even to *talk* about outside the box. How could she possibly think they'd be open to anything like applying lessons from Navy football to the business? What was she thinking? This was no football team, and she was no Shafe.

CHAPTER 5

All Things Digital

EARLY IN THE AFTERNOON, AIMEE WAS GOING OVER CLIENT files in her office when she heard a knock on her door. Without pause it swung open and Conroy strode in. *Just great,* she thought as she started to gather herself.

"So, Aimee. I guess you're wondering what all the mystery is about," Conroy said smugly.

Aimee was immediately on guard, sensing that she was on thin ice. She needed to better understand the politics of what was going on, so she played along. "I take it you've got an exciting proposal to talk about," she returned brightly.

"Actually, it's a lot more than just a proposal. But yes, it's very exciting. The board gave preliminary approval to the budget last week." Conroy started talking faster, the phrases spilling out on top of each other. "That's what the webinar you missed was all about: how modern-thinking companies are shifting their sales model to the Web, going all digital. Just think of the costs we'll save as we get rid of the sales reps and the archaic approach to sales. Each rep can handle only so many accounts, so we're really limited on how much we can grow. But with an all-digital model, the sky's the limit."

"Whoa. Back up a minute. Get rid of the sales reps? What do you mean? All of them?" Aimee's jaw dropped.

"Well, not all at once. We need to transition, of course. And we'll need to hold on to a few in each region to handle special situations. But—"

"You're kidding, right?" Aimee still couldn't wrap her head around what Conroy was telling her. It sounded crazy. But she knew she had to tread carefully. The ambush meeting with Faith was still fresh in her mind. *What were they thinking? Were they thinking at all?* It seemed to her that Conroy was taking the top-down approach to the worst possible extreme. If she didn't stop this soon, Calara would have no front line and its position in the marketplace would be in serious jeopardy. It was time for her to draw a battle line—win or lose.

"I'm sorry, Conroy. I didn't mean to reply so harshly. Certainly, we always need to innovate and avoid becoming stagnant in our approach if we're going to stay ahead of the competition. You've just caught me by surprise," Aimee said, trying to recover. "As your head of sales, I need to understand what the plan is and how it's going to work out for our key customers. Can you walk me through it?" She instinctively knew that keeping the focus on customers and not on the internal plan was safer and more fruitful ground. Her approach fell in line with "Start with the end in mind," one of the points she had picked up from studying Stephen Covey.

"I know you don't like me, Aimee, but I'm willing to set that aside. Faith and Ian seem to think your experience with customers could help, especially during the early transition. That's why they asked me to talk to you—to get you on board."

Aimee noted Conroy's "set that aside" comment, which she was savvy enough to know meant "as long as you give up and do things my way."

Instead of telling Conroy what she thought of him and his half-baked plan, Aimee just smiled and said, "Well, there's certainly a lot to think about. What kind of timing are we talking about here?"

Aimee tried to keep her face expressionless while her mind churned. *Customers. Customers are the key—the one element we have to focus on above everything else.* How could she convince Conroy and the others that you can't focus on customers if you don't have anyone to focus on them?

"Aimee, you have to know that we're at a turning point. The future is here now. I know you're kind of old school—"

"Old school?" Aimee couldn't help but react sharply. "What's that supposed to mean?"

"Down, girl, take it easy. Nothing personal."

Aimee was fuming inside. *Two huge, personal insults in five seconds. That has to be some kind of world record!* But she kept her emotions in check and didn't speak another word. She knew that anything she said would hurt her cause. In fact, she might lose the war before she even got to the first battle. Inwardly she smiled at the irony. She believed in the power of her frontline people, and here she was thinking about wars and battles. This was not a battle with a front line. This was a battle to save the front line.

"It's your decision. We all have to either get on board or get out of the way." Conroy shrugged and turned to leave. "We'll talk more later, after you've had a chance to think this through."

As the door closed behind him, Aimee's shoulders sagged. She didn't know whether to cry, to scream, or to pound the desk in frustration. *How could everything have gotten so far off course so fast?*

She straightened up. She knew where to start looking for answers.

⋮

Aimee took a deep breath as she sat down across from Ian, who was busy behind his large mahogany desk.

"Ian, thanks for squeezing me in on such short notice," Aimee said. Her tone was firm and her shoulders were squared.

"To be honest Aimee, I was expecting you," Ian returned in his soft, always pragmatic style. "The changes that Conroy is spearheading are moving quite rapidly." Ian paused to gage Aimee's reaction.

Aimee did not provide her usual rapid retort. Instead she took a breath and reminded herself that composure was paramount to reach Ian.

"Ian, Conroy issued me an ultimatum yesterday. I need to know if he did so with your blessing."

"No, I am not aware of any ultimatum," Ian answered matter-of-factly. His brow betrayed his words, however, and Aimee could tell her question had caught him off guard. "What sort of ultimatum did Conroy present?"

"Fire the sales team and join him in his digital revolution, or get out of his way—by leaving the company. I'm paraphrasing a little, but Conroy's message was clear." As she finished the sentence, Aimee drew strength from the fact that she had not gotten choked up or angry, as she feared she might.

"Aimee, let me be clear. No one is suggesting that you leave the company. If Conroy implied that in any way, he was out of line."

Aimee had Ian on the defensive, exactly what she needed. "Ian, I took to heart your comments when you and Faith met with me in my office. You ended that discussion by telling me that the company needs me."

"Yes. I believe that wholeheartedly."

"Ian, I agree with you. The company does need me—the sales force needs me to help them get back on track and stand up to this plan that Conroy is pushing, which will be disastrous if implemented. Do you really think that Calara can be successful in our market with no sales force?"

Before Ian could respond, Aimee continued "Ian, I am not going to sit idly by and watch Conroy destroy us, much less jump in to help him."

"Aimee, Faith and I were clear that we are moving forward with the digital marketing plan. Support is lining up for board approval." Ian's retort was intended to slow Aimee's assault.

"But the board doesn't meet with customers, Ian," Aimee volleyed back, showing no signs of retreating. "I came back to this company because I love what we do. I love how we help our customers solve problems that are real and unique to them. The company does need me; it needs me as an advocate for our customers!"

The emotion that Aimee had held in check to this point began to show as her voice cracked and her breathing visibly accelerated. She took another deep breath and gathered her thoughts. *Keep the focus on the customer, not the digital plan*, she thought. *The plan should follow the focus, not the other way around.* If she argued about the plan, it would be an uphill battle. But if she fought for doing what's right for the customers, she was on safer ground.

"Aimee, I am not going to stop the digital initiative, but that said, do you have something you would like to suggest?" Ian offered.

"I do."

"Well?"

"The board has heard only one side of the story. I would like to present an alternative view."

"What do you mean, 'alternative view'?"

"I mean that this company has been built in large part on the back—on the sweat—of the sales team. People like Joe Fabri. Richard should know that, though he seems to have forgotten."

Ian did not immediately respond, so Aimee continued.

"We cannot simply disband our sales team and hope to stay connected to our customers. Any new approach to sales has got to blend their frontline experience and know-how if we want to reach the next level. The board members have to understand the impact of such a decision, and I want to be the one to tell them."

Aimee knew Ian had always liked her, and her willingness to shoot straight and put it all on the line was the chief reason behind his admiration. She could tell by the skeptical look on his face that it would be hard to persuade him to allow her to present her ideas directly to the board. She also realized that the sales team's recent performance did little to bolster her position.

Ian shook his head. "You know I can't let you go directly to the board. What are you proposing?"

Aimee pounced. "I'd like your approval to meet with Richard—and you—directly. I'll put together a proposal for how to turn sales around. If I can convince you and Richard that what I am saying has merit, then we can give the board a more comprehensive plan to consider. An alternative, Ian—that's all I ask.

Let me give the board an alternative to slashing the sales force to consider."

"All right. Let me check with Richard's admin and see when we can meet. You can have your shot. Although, Aimee, I have to be honest, I don't think there is much you can say to change the direction we're heading."

"That's fair. I...we just need a shot. What we do with it is up to us."

Ian smiled and added, "The company needs you, regardless of the direction we choose."

As Aimee processed the immediate consequences of her successful pleas, she decided to press for one more concession. "What about Conroy and his list of sales rep terminations? Faith told me he wants them done by the end of the month, and that is fast approaching."

"No promises, but I will talk to Faith. Maybe we can find a way to improve the quarterly numbers without having to initiate the terminations immediately—or at least reduce the number in this wave."

"I appreciate that, Ian. Thanks for your time, and thanks for hearing me out."

Aimee and Ian stood. There was nothing else to say. It was obvious to Aimee they were both satisfied with the conversation, but she was afraid they had radically different views of the benefits this delay would deliver.

CHAPTER 6

The Bike Ride

Aimee pulled out of the parking lot, glad that the week was finally ending. She needed some time to process her thoughts and sort them out. Too many things were happening too fast. She needed to try to make sense of everything and figure out her next move.

As she merged onto the Washington beltway and joined the rest of the Friday evening rush toward home, she was just starting to relax when her phone rang. She rolled her eyes. *What now?*

A quick glance at the console revealed that it was Joe. She breathed a sigh of relief and punched the Accept button.

"Hey, Joe. Heading home?"

"Not quite yet, Aimee." She tensed at the sound of his voice. This was definitely not the cheerful Joe she had anticipated hearing.

"What's wrong?" she asked. "Mr. Cameron didn't call back with more problems on the account, did he?"

"No. Nothing that simple," Joe continued. "I just left Conroy's office."

Aimee's head rocked back as she took a deep breath. The conversation paused as she realized she was clenching the wheel and slowing down. "Really?" She tried to sound relaxed. "And what was that about?"

"He's offered me a new role at the company. Turns out my current position may not exist much longer. I'm not sure I really took it all in. But I guess we're joining the bandwagon and going digital, whatever that means." From Joe's tone, Aimee heard his unspoken questions: *Are you in on this? Why didn't you warn me, Aimee?*

The last thing she needed was for Joe to defect. *What an underhanded move by Conroy.* Aimee composed her thoughts rather than blurting out what she really wanted to say. "I'm not entirely sure about all the plans at this point, Joe. What kind of role did Conroy offer you?"

"I don't think he really knows yet, but it won't be customer facing and it won't be commissioned. But at least I'll still have a job. He says he wants to take advantage of my years of experience, you know."

"Joe, you still have a job. I don't care what Conroy said. No one's taking your job away." Aimee forced out each syllable as she tried to be reassuring, but it was impossible, as the circumstances caused her to doubt her own words.

"That's not the way it sounded to me, Aimee. Conroy was pretty clear that only a few of the sales reps would be offered new positions. He talked about messaging, segmentation, digital platforms, and all that. I don't know much about that stuff, but I know I'm not in a position to retire just yet."

"Slow down, Joe." Aimee was fuming but stayed professional and maintained her composure. "Give me some time to figure out what's going on."

"I'm not sure I can, Aimee. Conroy wants an answer the first of next week. I don't think I can put him off for very long."

"Just avoid him on Monday. You need to be in the field anyhow. Call and set up an appointment to talk to him late Tuesday. That should give me enough time to figure this out."

"Okay." Aimee could hear the sigh in Joe's voice as he abruptly wrapped up: "Talk to you Monday, Aimee. Bye."

The line went silent just as traffic came to a halt. "I hate this beltway! What's wrong with all these people? Can't they just—" She slammed both palms into the steering wheel as she bit her lip.

⋮

By the time she pulled into her driveway, Aimee had reached a decision. She grabbed her phone and took a deep breath to steady her voice. Then she hit the redial button and waited for Joe.

Come on, Joe. Pick up.

"I thought it might be you." Joe sounded both relieved and apprehensive.

"I don't need a couple of days, Joe. The reason I rejoined the company was clear, and nothing has happened to change my mind." With each word she spoke, Aimee was picking up speed and confidence. "We both know this company will always be built on a foundation of strong customer relationships. And the only way to build and maintain those relationships is face to face. We can't just put up a pretty web page and expect customers to flock to us. We have to—"

"Hold on, Aimee. I'm on your side. No need to convince me. I was just waiting to make sure you weren't leaving me hanging. If you're there, I'm with you—all the way." The apprehensive tone of Joe's voice had faded and only relief was left.

Aimee relaxed. "Great! I was really worried that you were going over to the dark side."

Joe laughed. "I thought I might have to, even though it's no place I want to be."

Then Joe turned serious, "Look, Aimee. I'm with you on this. I'm all in. As long as I know you're still on the team, I want you to know that you can count on me. You know I believe in tried-and-true relationship selling, and I'm not eager to throw that away to make way for any newfangled digital replacement."

Joe's confidence in her humbled Aimee. Her faith in Calara and the people of Calara was restored for the moment. She took a deep breath to thwart the nervous uncertainty over what they clearly faced.

Joe continued, "In fact, I'll go ahead and send Conroy an e-mail and tell him what he can do with his offer. Tactfully and professionally, of course."

Aimee could hear the smile in Joe's voice, and it brought a smile to her face—for a moment easing her anxiety about the battle that lay ahead of them.

"Take care, Aimee. Have a great weekend. Get out for one of those bike rides like you and Bill used to do and figure out how we win this thing."

"Sure thing, Joe. I'll do that." Aimee hoped her voice sounded more sure than she felt. "You have a great weekend, too. I'll see you Monday, and we'll get to work putting this whole mess behind us and get back to our customers."

"Bye."

After Joe hung up, Aimee sat motionless in the driveway, collecting her thoughts and trying to put the week behind her. She hated bringing stress from work into her home. Just then she looked at the picture window in the living room and saw Kylie's smiling face as she pointed to her mom's car, all the while braced in the arms of Marc. Aimee waved and opened the car door, pushing the call to the back of her mind.

⋮

Though the horizon was visible, exposing the distant tree line and hinting at a crisp blue sky, the sun was still twenty minutes from gracing the day. Aimee loved this time of day, especially when she was at the front end of a long Saturday bike ride. As she pulled her shiny new "baby" from the garage, her eye caught a glimpse of her "old ride," the bike she had purchased when Bill was introducing her to the sport. Thank goodness Bill had taken the time to coach her to see the beauty of an exhilarating morning ride. This morning Aimee was looking forward to the ride more than usual. She had not slept well. Conroy's tactics, Faith's changed demeanor, and Ian's narrow-mindedness pressed on her in a way that she was not accustomed to. She was unsettled; she didn't like this feeling, this lack of a clear path forward.

The first few miles were over before Aimee knew it. Her cadence was natural, her breathing had become relaxed, and with the fresh oxygen her mind began to clear. She had gone out on a limb to persuade Joe to join her on this crazy quest to restore performance excellence for the sales team. As he has done so many times before, Joe stepped out on the ledge with her. This time it was different, though. This time they were playing for all the marbles. If she was wrong, if she couldn't pull it off, she would take Joe down with her. She was young enough to survive the blow. But Joe would likely have a difficult time rebounding and establishing himself with a new company after such a fall. Could she really flip the tables? Could she lead Joe, the sales team, and the rest of the company away from the cliff that Conroy was marching them toward?

Ah, the hill. Her focus turned to the road in front of her. She loved this part of the ride. She smiled as she remembered how she used to dread it. Now it was "her" hill: a steady seven-degree, four-mile climb that marked the halfway point on her regular Saturday route.

She shifted to the middle ring of her gears and increased her pedaling cadence. She decided to attack the hill and push herself to capacity rather than take it easy. Her gloved right fingers pushed the shift lever to drop down one sprocket on the rear cluster of gears, and she started concentrating on her pedal stroke, spinning faster, keeping pressure on the pedals all the way around the stroke. Her speed held steady.

She concentrated more on wiping the mud off her shoes at the bottom of the stroke, grateful for the clipless pedals Bill had insisted she get. With her feet firmly attached to the pedals, she could power them all the way around, not just mash down on them. The hill turned up just a bit. Aimee responded by dropping down one more gear. A quick check of her heart-rate monitor showed 85 percent, approaching the red zone. Aimee smiled and leaned down lower over the handlebars.

Today she owned the hill. The sun broke free of the horizon. She could feel the unusual warmth for this time in October. The sweat was running freely from her brow as her heart rate pushed up into the red zone. Aimee loved a challenge. She loved how she felt when she and her bike joined seamlessly to produce the feeling of accomplishment she was after. And each time she beat this hill, she felt a reassuring sense of satisfaction.

Aimee sought this same sense of accomplishment at work. The desire to build on earlier successes at her job is what drove her to rejoin Calara Enterprises. Though she played hard to get when Bill called her, she really wanted to conquer the challenge that she felt she had not completed before starting a family.

The crest of the hill was in sight now. She focused her eyes on that crest, shifted up two clicks, and stood up on the pedals. *This hill is mine, yeah!*

Thoughts of Conroy, Faith, and all the difficulties at work evaporated from her mind. Her mission was clear. Crest the hill. She sprinted the last fifty yards, cleared the top, and started accelerating down the back side of the hill, quickly reaching thirty miles per hour, settling down low in the drop handlebars to decrease wind resistance.

If only she could own the situation at work. If only she could somehow see a clear path to stop Conroy's plan. The company's abrupt shift in direction was the last thing Aimee expected as she walked into her new office four short months ago. Sales were down, but the team seemed strong and Bill was working on the issue. Bill appeared fully in control. And the joy of reengaging with Joe was like meeting your favorite uncle at the family reunion. But now there was no Bill. Now she felt totally and suddenly responsible for Joe's future. It certainly wasn't clear to her how she could beat this hill at work. Right now she didn't even have an idea of how long the climb was. Conroy's plan ignored the one key ingredient that has always driven her: *people.*

She needed a sure way to focus the activities of the sales team to drive business results. The fact that she had no answer for the question mark in her journal caused an uneasy burning in her mind. It was similar to the burning in her lungs when she worked to crest a new and challenging hill for the first time. She resolved to do the one tactic she had learned as a cyclist: keep pedaling, keep moving forward.

CHAPTER 7

Like Coaching Football

MONDAYS ALWAYS SEEMED TO BE FILLED WITH ENDLESS meetings. This Monday was particularly frustrating as Aimee was internally wrestling with how to deal with Conroy and his plan. With little progress on this front, this had been one long, pointless, and frustrating day. *I can't wait to get out of here and head for home*, Aimee thought as she found herself watching the clock at seven minutes before three.

As she stared aimlessly across at the clock, tirelessly ticking, she allowed herself to think the one thought she had put off: maybe she'd made a big mistake coming back to Calara. She'd given it her best shot, but maybe it just wasn't going to work. Taking so much time off from the corporate scene left her out of touch, and she just couldn't seem to reconnect with the company. She hated that feeling. The energy that she had thrived on in the past was gone. Maybe she wasn't a good fit for the new Calara. And if she had to sit through one more meeting with Conroy, her head would explode. *What a blow-hard. What a conniving—* Aimee stopped short; even in these silent musings she didn't like to think ill of others. *But Conroy—he really gets under my skin in every way.*

Aimee's internal rant was broken by the ding and flash of a meeting reminder on her idle computer screen.

"Oh no," she said out loud. "My meeting with Shafe! I totally forgot it." She had set the reminder to 3:00 p.m., leaving her just enough drive time to get to the field as practice was breaking up.

Even as she started to shut down the computer and pack up, she weighed whether she should waste Shafe's time on what must be a silly, and probably hopeless, notion. Maybe she should just call him and say she couldn't make it. *Why drive all the way over to Annapolis now? This crazy idea is done. In fact, I think I'm done.*

She pulled her phone from her purse and stared at it as she thought through what she would say to Shafe. No matter what opening line she thought of, she knew she wouldn't make it past the sound of Shafe's confident voice booming back at her through the phone, "What? Why?" She knew that he was no quitter and would only scoff at the little pity party she was throwing for herself. "All the more reason for you to get over here! Right now!"

The corners of her mouth betrayed the small upturn of a smile, something that had been noticeably absent these last few days. Her big brother had always had this effect on her. It wasn't so much the words he said as the way he said them. He had confidence galore—enough to share with everyone. So much that it seemed to jump from his body to hers.

She could hear him now: "You know what Vince says." Shafe was always quoting his hero, Vince Lombardi. "Winners never quit and quitters never win." How many times had she heard that growing up? The small upturn across her lips blossomed into a full-fledged smile. Aimee realized she was completely relaxed with a refreshing sense of calm. Maybe Shafe's positive mojo from the football team can transfer to her. Well, she had nothing to lose.

I'm going to learn how to play Navy football, she thought with a chuckle as she rushed out the door of her office.

⋮

The drive passed quickly as Aimee tried to think through the situation from every possible angle, but it still wasn't clear. And she still wasn't convinced that Shafe's football expertise would be able to help. She turned into the parking lot next to the practice field. As she got out of the car, a midshipman walking by greeted her with a snappy "Good afternoon, ma'am."

Ugh. Every time she visited the Academy, these young guys made her feel like an old woman.

It wasn't long before Aimee spotted her brother in the distance wrapping up his practice session with the offensive linemen. Shafe was not a particularly large man by football standards, but he managed to stand out among Navy's group of linemen.

As Aimee walked across the field toward Shafe, the autumn smell of fresh-cut grass was impossible to avoid. The smell brought her back to simple days of high school football, where Friday's competition was the crosstown rival and the winners and losers were clearly displayed by the final configuration of small yellow lights arranged on a weathered black scoreboard. If only competition in her professional life were as straightforward.

Before reaching Shafe, Aimee's trek across the field was interrupted by a stranger who had all the trappings of a beat reporter for a newspaper.

"Are you with the *Star*?"

"Pardon me?" Aimee replied.

"Haven't seen you here before. Are you the new reporter for the *Star*?"

"I'm sorry. I don't quite follow."

"My apologies. I'm Ryan. I follow Navy football for the *Annapolis Capital*. I assumed you were here for the coach's post-practice comments."

"Oh no," Aimee retorted. "My brother, Shafe, is the offensive line coach. This is the only time he could spare."

"I bet. Shafe must be busy. The whole staff is heads down preparing for the upcoming game against Notre Dame." Then with a clumsy pause the reporter added, "You don't have insight on Notre Dame's defensive scheme for the game, do you? Must be important for you to trek out here to talk to him in person."

"Don't I wish I knew some insights!" Aimee smiled. "No, I'm just here to pick my brother's brain on how he drives top performance from his linemen. I'm trying to translate some of that approach to my work with our sales team."

"That sounds like a stretch," Ryan replied as he furrowed his brow. "Big sweaty linemen mowing each other down versus well-groomed, polite sales staff? I don't follow."

"I know, I know."

The reporter stood and shrugged. "Well, going to fill me in? What's the connection?"

This guy's kind of pushy. Guess it comes with the job, Aimee thought. But then she figured, what the heck? Here's a chance to test the idea on someone who seems bright and inquisitive.

"I have a notion. Are you sure you really want to hear this?"

He shrugged again. "Nothing better to do. Coach Price is running late. And, hey, I might learn something."

"I'm not quite sure how to express this yet, but... Well, let me start with a question: do you think that Navy has a chance in its game against Notre Dame?"

"Honestly? About as much as a snowball's chance in—you know. But don't tell your brother. I don't want a guy like that mad at me."

Aimee chuckled. "That was quick. Why so certain?"

"Look at the Notre Dame roster—size and raw talent," Ryan stated with flat certainty.

"What about two years ago? Navy beat Notre Dame. That means it is clearly possible."

The reporter's reply dripped sarcasm: "Sure. One out of forty-three tries isn't so bad."

"But Shafe tells me that Navy's program is different now. The way they prepare and the way they train each position is different. The clarity in what they practice has changed, too. Maybe the last win wasn't such a fluke at all."

"Yeah, right. Just Google Notre Dame's roster. Evaluate their players' size. Do it before you place any bets. And what does any of this have to do with helping the sales team at your company?"

"For starters, we're like Navy in that we are not the top tier company in our industry, so we have difficulty recruiting against the big guys to staff our sales force. Sales have been down recently, and some in our company want to shut down the sales team altogether and use those dollars to fund a digital marketing campaign. They have concluded that our sales team can't compete."

"Sounds reasonable. Maybe they are right. Digital is the way the world is going. I think it's time to read the writing on the wall."

"Not so fast," Aimee countered. It felt good to spar like this. "I think an important element isn't being considered, and it's that we've lost sight of how we prepare our salespeople. I wonder if we're focusing on the right things. I think that we haven't been clear on what we're asking the sales staff to do and, by default, haven't been preparing them well for the competition that they face. The thing is, I'm running out of runway to change our path. That's why I'm standing out here on a football field—getting in line to get a few minutes with my brother."

"Your brother has the answer?"

"He believes that the fundamental philosophy that Navy uses, the approach that he uses for the offensive line, can be applied to our sales force."

"And what is that?"

"You don't know? I thought you covered Navy football."

"We don't talk much about philosophy. We talk mostly about who's starting, what the coach is happy with in regard to last week's game, and what he hopes to change for this week's game. Again, compare the rosters of Navy and Notre Dame. It comes down to size and talent."

"I think there's something here, or Shafe wouldn't have insisted that he and I meet. There has to be something."

"I now know where Shafe gets his optimism from. Sorry to say it, but I think the odds for your sales team are about the same as Navy's against Notre Dame." The reporter chuckled as he turned away to catch one of the coaching staff walking by.

Thanks for nothing, Aimee thought wryly.

"There you are!" Aimee turned at the sound of her brother's voice. He was smiling as he approached her from the far sideline.

Maybe that reporter's right. Maybe I shouldn't even waste Shafe's time with such an out-there idea anyway. Doubt uncontrollably rose in her throat. Aimee hated this feeling and hated even more to appear weak in front of her brother. She turned her head and cleared her throat.

"So, let's talk more about this idea of how to get your sales team to perform." It was typical of Shafe to pick up right where they had left off. "Want to hear where I'm coming from?"

"Absolutely. Whatever you're doing sure has made a difference for Navy on the football field. So what's the secret?"

"I have to admit, we've become quite competitive. And, you know what? The game is a lot more fun when the other team is more worried about us than we are about them. Some of the teams that were all too happy to schedule us as an easy win are now refusing to put us on their schedules. And frankly, a lot of that change starts with the offensive line."

"Getting a little cocky there, aren't we, Big Brother?"

"It's not cocky when you earn it," Shafe countered. "Anyway, I should explain a couple of key concepts about how we think about performance for the linemen. First, and most importantly, we have a clear definition of the role each lineman plays in the offense."

"Yeah, like knock the other guy down? These are linemen we're talking about, right?"

"Don't let stereotypes cloud your thinking, Sis. In fact, we use this same idea for every position on the team. By 'role,' I mean that we're very clear to each of our guys about exactly what we want him to do. We're a lot more specific than just 'knock someone down.' In fact, it's a lot more specific than run block or pass block. Every position has a clear and important role. And those roles are designed for the team to succeed. If everyone performs his role, then we have a pretty good shot at winning our fair share of the plays."

"What do you mean?" Aimee thought for a second. "Oh, you mean like in cycling? The role of most riders on a cycling team is to help just one or two riders advance out of the pack and cross the finish line first."

"Exactly. You got it," Shafe exclaimed. "Each player on the field has a role just like that. But it doesn't begin with the result; it begins by breaking down exactly how we intend to win the game. Our strategy for winning is unique to us, so the roles we define for our linemen are different from those defined by, well, Notre Dame, for example. As for your situation, remember how I said that revenue is the wrong measure?"

"Yeah. But I'm still not sure what you mean by that. That's what sales is all about—producing revenue. Just like football is all about scoring the most points."

"Ah, but that's only part of the story. And not the most important part given Navy's strategy for winning games."

Aimee looked skeptical. "So how do you win games without scoring points?"

"You don't, silly. But if we focus just on scoring points, we usually don't win. Think about it. Navy isn't the biggest, the fastest, or the most athletic team in the NCAA. Some teams out there can run up the score like nobody's business. If we get into a shootout with them, we'll lose every time."

"So what do you focus on?" Aimee leaned in, listening intently.

"Actually, it's pretty simple. Our key goal for every drive is to keep the ball as long as possible and to score something. In fact, we measure game performance on both the amount of time we keep the ball and the percentage of possessions on which we score. Put another way, we hold the ball a lot more than the other guys, and if we score the majority of the times we have the ball, we have a pretty good chance to win."

Something in Aimee's mind started to click. "Go on. I'm getting it."

Shafe continued. "Let's talk about that revenue idea some more. What's the real goal of your sales force? What's your equivalent of time holding the ball? Size of each sale? Market share? Or maybe—"

Aimee jumped in: "Relationships! Besides revenue, our key performance measure is the depth of our relationships."

"Okay—sounds great," Shafe said. "Now dig deeper and explain to me how that relates to your success."

"Well," Aimee began slowly, building up speed and excitement as her thinking jelled. "Our biggest successes come when we can establish a great long-term, trusted relationship with a customer. Then that customer will continue to buy from us year after year. If we focus on a short-term sales win, then we don't seem to do as well over the long haul. Just like Navy. If you score too fast, you let the other team back on the field. In our case, if we bring a short-term perspective without focusing on relationships, then customers start to look around at our competitors and we end up having to cut our prices to keep those customers happy. Or worse, we lose them entirely and have to try to win them back later."

Aimee suddenly looked puzzled again. "But what does this new definition of success have to do with roles?"

"Everything," Shafe told her. "Once we understand exactly what we need to do to win the game, we can design each role to contribute to how we win."

Aimee's thoughts flashed back to the question mark in her journal. This is the answer. *This is how people are connected to the desired results.*

"Let's back up a sec," Shafe said. "In its simplest form, Navy runs only two plays: option left and option right. The defense knows the play as the ball is snapped. How can we possibly hope to be successful in a situation like that? Well, without going into too much detail, each lineman executes a particular blocking scheme based on the formation that the defense has lined up in. The linemen don't block the same way each time the option play is called because they block in a way that takes advantage of the specific defensive formation. The quarterback then reads the results of the block and decides which runner to give the ball to or keeps it himself. The result is a dramatic and split-second dance that occurs on each and every option play. As the defense shifts its approach, the blocking scheme and the handoff decision shift accordingly."

"Okay, you lost me there—sounds complicated." Aimee mused. "I really like to watch Navy play, but I'm not sure I understood what you said."

"I'm not surprised. Honestly, it took me a full season to understand the blocking schemes to the point where I could be good at teaching them to our incoming linemen each year. The point is not for you to learn the blocking schemes but rather for you to understand how we break our schemes down so that we can establish standards of excellence for each play."

"Okay, I'm all ears."

"First, we know what outcome we want the lineman to produce against each defensive scheme.

"Second, we make sure that each lineman understands the techniques to achieve that outcome. And third, we have the linemen relentlessly practice in a coached environment. They practice both the techniques and when to use them until executing the proper technique becomes second nature."

"You make it sound so easy," Aimee said, feeling encouraged.

"I would say it is simple but not necessarily easy," Shafe returned with the quiet confidence of one who has lived the ups and downs of teaching young football players the "Navy way."

"Okay, I think I'm following you. I need to be clear on what outcomes matter to our sales team, teach them the techniques to produce these outcomes, and then practice and coach them to perfection." Aimee's voice betrayed the enthusiasm she was beginning to feel.

"Do these three things, Aimee, and I'm confident that you can turn around the performance of your sales team," Shafe assured his younger sister. "Here comes Coach Price. Let me introduce you." Coach Price was in his fifth year at Navy, having turned around a program that saw only one win the year before he arrived. With Navy's success, both he and the triple-option offense he implemented had gained notoriety and respect among the college football establishment.

"Shafe, before he gets here, I have one more question." Aimee decided to bring up the conversation she'd just had with the newspaper reporter, seeing as he seemed so confident in his opinions.

"I was talking to that reporter over there, and he doesn't believe that Navy can beat Notre Dame in the upcoming game. He challenged me to go online and compare the size of the Navy offensive linemen versus that of Notre Dame." Aimee felt doubt creeping back in.

"Hold that thought," Shafe said as he hailed the coach.

"Hi, Coach. I'd like you to meet my sister, Aimee. She has some questions on how we train our football players to be competitive against the notable opponents on our schedule."

"Hi, Shafe. Nice to meet you, Aimee. I just walked over to find out who this strange face belonged to. Aimee, you didn't go to Notre Dame, did you? You aren't here spying on our game preps, are you?" Coach Price questioned Aimee half-jokingly.

"Absolutely not, Coach. Wouldn't dream of it. My veins run with Navy blue and gold," Aimee returned earnestly with the pride of a dedicated fan.

"Someone . . . um . . . that reporter, Ryan, I think, has planted a seed of doubt in Aimee's mind about whether we can win our upcoming game with Notre Dame. Something to do with comparing the size of the offensive lines. Care to comment on that, Coach?" Shafe taunted lightheartedly.

"Oh, let me see. You mean the fact that Notre Dame's line outweighs ours by an average of thirty-two pounds per man? The implication, of course, is that we're not big enough to play in the big time. Is this what causes your doubt, young lady?" The question obviously hit a nerve with Coach Price.

"I think that's what the reporter was referring to. A thirty-two-pound difference—is this a lot?"

"You bet it's a lot. Those who don't know our system often point to this or other size statistics to write off our chances of victory. What they don't tell you is that the size of our line is intentional, not accidental."

"Sorry, Coach. I was just repeating a conversation I had with that reporter over there." Aimee pointed to Ryan, who was walking off the field.

"Ah, Ryan—the ultimate skeptic. Well, for a reporter whose job is supposed to be digging for new angles, he can be a bit shallow and full of conventional thinking. We have studied the offensive line in depth to understand not only what we want the players to do but to identify the profile of the lineman who does it best."

"Wait a minute, Coach. You intentionally recruit small linemen? Shouldn't you be trying to compete for the biggest and strongest players you can get?" Aimee's questions came from thoughts of tying this conversation back to her sales force.

"Great question, young lady, and no, we don't look for small linemen. We look for the right linemen. Our triple-option offense relies on speed and quickness, so our recruiting and training target speed and explosiveness. In fact, our entire off-season strength program is built on this goal." Coach Price was clearly proud of the results Navy's football program had achieved since he arrived. Right now, however, he appeared focused on Notre Dame. He gave her a nod as he began to head for the locker room.

"Stop by my office, Shafe. I want to discuss their left defensive end. He's pro material, and I want to make sure we are on the same page about how to handle him," Coach Price said. He looked back at Aimee. "Nice to meet you. I'll have Shafe give you a copy of the book I insist our coaches read. You'll get a lot out of it. The principles in this book have changed every aspect of our system. Remember, worthwhile training is always focused on a specific outcome."

"Thanks, Coach. Good luck against Notre Dame." Aimee was glad that that little exchange was over and was eager to get back to her car and capture her thoughts in her journal.

After giving a quick goodbye hug to her brother, Aimee sprinted back to her car. Sitting in the parking lot with the driver's door still open, Aimee flipped open her journal to the page with her question mark. Coach Price's last words were still ringing in her ears: "Worthwhile training is always focused on a specific outcome."

She wrote the last word slowly—"Outcome." *But what if we have more than one outcome?* She quickly added five check boxes as if she were starting a list, underlined the word, and added an *s* to form "Outcomes."

She stared at the page while recounting her brother's discussion of the importance of understanding what the desired results are at Calara. Just over the word "Results" Aimee inserted "Business," and to the right of her question mark Aimee penned "Clear outcomes that link people to desired business results." She then traced over the word "Outcomes," underlining it multiple times for emphasis.

This made sense. It felt natural and totally aligned with her belief that people are the key to driving results.

Now only one thing was missing: the outcomes.

How, she wondered, *do I figure out the right outcomes for our sales team?*

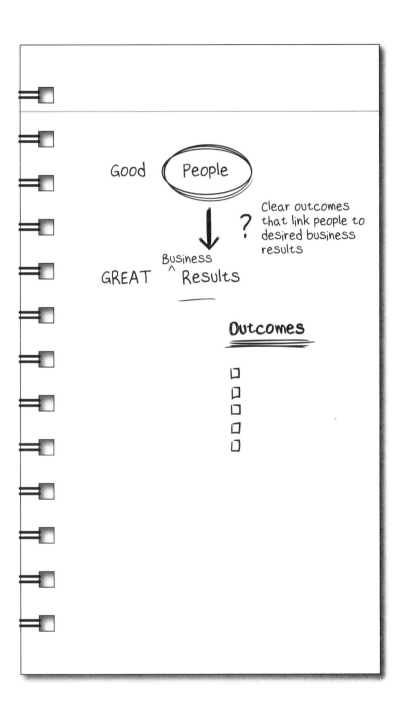

CHAPTER 8

The Book

Aimee pulled into the driveway and sighed, realizing she was late arriving home again. *Seems like late is my new normal.* This day had been a long and drawn-out one. Yesterday's visit with Shafe seemed like eons ago. She sighed again as she walked up the front steps and reached for the doorknob, bracing herself for her husband's reaction.

"Hi, Aim," Marc said.

Wow, that's a relief! thought Aimee, hearing the good mood in his voice. Maybe she wasn't in trouble after all.

"You just missed him."

"Missed who?" Aimee asked.

"Your brother—Shafe. He stopped by to say hi."

Crud, I knew I was late. "When did he leave?"

"Just about ten minutes ago. He waited as long as he could but said he had to get home." Aimee sensed a touch of sarcasm in Marc's voice. Maybe he really was upset at how late she was.

"But he left something for you on the kitchen table. Some book he said you wanted to read."

Aimee walked into the kitchen and saw the book on the table, not far from the plates Marc and Kylie had used for dinner. The clean plate reserved for her rested nearby. It stung to realize just what she was missing out on at home.

She picked up the book, delighted that Shafe had passed it along so quickly, and read the title out loud: *Exemplary Performance*. She saw a note sticking out of the book.

"What?" Aimee realized Marc was telling her something. "I'm sorry. I didn't hear you."

"I said, Kylie and I have already eaten. But we saved you some. Here, let me heat it up for you."

Aimee smiled, confused again, not at all sure how to read Marc.

She opened the book and read the note from Shafe.

> Remember, Aimee, it's all about the outcomes. Forget about the rest until you understand the outcomes. Success will follow! Hugs, S

"Here you go, Aimee." Marc set a plate of chicken fried rice, a spring roll, and some chopsticks on the table. "Sit down and read your book."

Aimee smiled at Marc and then turned her attention to the table of contents, missing the roll of Marc's eyes as he turned and walked away.

"Thanks, honey," she said and sat down to start reading.

⋮

Aimee felt Marc shaking her. "Wake up, sleepyhead, and turn off that crazy alarm clock!"

She slowly emerged from her deep sleep and realized her alarm was going off. She hit the Off button and lay back down on her pillow.

Marc shook her again. "The alarm means it's time to get up, not time to lie back down. Let's go—time to start the weekend."

Aimee groaned and sat up.

"Did you stay up late last night reading again?"

"Not too late," Aimee lied, but the reminder was all she needed. Just thinking about the book again renewed her excitement about what she had learned. These few days had gone by quickly as she devoured the book Shafe had lent her, and now that she had finished it, she couldn't wait to get to the office and share this new approach with Faith. She knew she had the key she needed.

Then Aimee thought, *Why wait until Monday? Faith is an early riser; I can call her right now.*

Aimee grabbed her phone and punched Faith's name from her favorites list. Faith barely had time to say hello before Aimee launched into her speech.

"Faith. Listen. I've got it. It's so exciting. Outcomes—focusing on outcomes is the key to improving sales." Aimee was pacing, holding the phone in one hand and the book in the other. "And it's not that complicated. We can—"

"Aimee, Aimee, Aimee. Stop right there. Listen."

"What?" Aimee was brought up short. "Faith, we've got the answer—"

"No, Aimee," Faith said in a way that invited no discussion. "You may have the answer, but you've got the wrong question. The question you should be asking is are you on board or not?"

"On board? On board with what?"

"On board with the digital transformation of Calara—that's what. The entire executive team is excited about where we're going and the possibilities for the future."

"What about you, Faith?" Aimee thought Faith sounded like she was reading from a prepared statement on the party line, not expressing her genuine thoughts. "You can't tell me you've bought into this crazy idea of wholesale abandonment of traditional sales practices."

"The idea is not crazy, Aimee. It's the future, and it's here. And yes, I have bought into it, as you say. I'm excited about what it means to our industry, our company, and our team. But look," Faith hesitated, "I'll keep an open mind to what you have to say about your output or outcome or whatever it is. Ian has already committed to letting you present your proposal before we proceed with layoffs. We'll listen—and then make our decision."

The hand that was holding the book dropped to Aimee's side. She was weeks away from having the data she needed to prove her point to Richard and Ian.

Faith continued. "But here's my advice to you: As you put together your presentation, think about the idea of a team and what it means to be on the team. Whatever we decide about the future of the company, you have to decide if you want to be on the team or not. Now, if you'll excuse me, I'm already late for an appointment."

"Sure. Thanks for taking my call, Faith. Have a good weekend."

Aimee looked at her phone, regretting the Saturday call. She wished that she had waited until Monday to talk with Faith face to face. But there was no time for regrets. Shifting gears, Aimee got up. It was time to get Kylie ready for their mother-daughter adventure so Marc could get a breather.

⋮

"Mommy! Where's my pumpkin?" Kylie inquired for the fifth time from her car seat in the Volvo.

"We put it in the back of the car, behind you, remember? We'll pull it out and put it on the front porch when we get home,"

Aimee responded, trying to be patient. The day with Kylie at the Homestead Gardens Fall Festival had totally exhausted Aimee. As she turned to check Kylie's acceptance of her answer, it was obvious that the day had drained Kylie of her seemingly boundless energy as well. Kylie was resting her head against the car seat, already fast asleep. The innocence in Kylie's face, as she sat without a care in the world, created a warm sense of contentment in Aimee.

In the pause initiated by Kylie's sleep, Aimee suddenly remembered that today was the big day, Navy versus Notre Dame. An image of Shafe pacing the sideline flashed through her mind as she reached to turn on the radio and quickly found the preset for 1430 WNAV. The hoarse and excited voice of the announcer instantly told her the results of the game before she even heard the words: "And for the second time in three years, Navy has defeated Notre Dame. This time 23 to 21 in a game that wasn't decided until the last two minutes. We're live in South Bend. Now let's join the press conference just outside Navy's locker room, where Coach Price is about to address the media."

The voice on the radio faded momentarily as Aimee thought of Shafe and tears welled in her eyes. She was proud of what Shafe had accomplished, proud to have him as a brother, and proud—and envious—of his persistent optimism regardless of the obstacles in front of him. The unique sound of Coach Price's voice snapped Aimee's attention back to the radio. She didn't really hear the question, but Coach Price's answer brought her back to their brief conversation on Navy's practice field.

"You know that our recruiting base is quite different from Notre Dame's. In fact, with no disrespect to any player on our team, we don't have a single superstar athlete on our roster. I'm not even sure how many of our players could make the Notre Dame team. That's not to say that we don't have good players. We have some very good players that have learned to be excellent in the role they play on the team. Each player is clear on the outcome he is responsible for during each and every play. Our coaching staff has created a robust system to identify excellence for each role, and then we focus our practices to achieve an unsurpassed level of excellence. And when each player achieves that level of excellence, success follows, as you saw today."

"Coach, are you saying that your squad practices harder than Notre Dame's?"

"Harder? No, I'm not saying that at all. But I am suggesting that we probably practice differently than they do—in part because we have to practice differently to be competitive."

"What about the final drive in the fourth quarter?"

That question made Aimee think about Calara's fourth quarter and the brief conversation with Faith earlier in the day. Faith just doesn't understand yet. Maybe it was true that we lost our focus on how we train and prepare our sales force, but with this new approach we can change that.

Coach Price's words and her readings from the book *Exemplary Performance* seemed to come together as she reflected. All at once, it was obvious to her what she must do next: find the outcomes that Joe and other stars like him produce!

Everything was starting to fall into place. Whether on the football field or in a cycling race, wins happen when all participants know the outcomes they are responsible for and produce those outcomes in each and every situation. The coaches have to make those outcomes clear and then design practice sessions to make sure each participant can excel at his or her position.

Sales is more like sports than she realized. Each member of the sales force has a role to play. And each role is responsible for a set of outcomes. When each person in a role produces those outcomes, then the sales team wins. So the job of sales leadership is to help all the team members understand exactly what outcomes they should produce and then coach them so they can excel. Wow! It all made sense. And if Navy could use that idea to beat the mighty Notre Dame, then Calara could certainly beat its competition as well.

Aimee pulled into the nearest convenience store parking lot to capture her thoughts. She wrote, "The outcomes are determined by figuring out what the best reps are already doing."

As soon as she got home and tucked Kylie in to finish her afternoon nap, she would send Joe an e-mail stressing the urgency for him to meet her for lunch early next week—and to bring the two sales reps that he respects the most. She had to do exactly as Coach Price outlined it. She would use the lunch to kick off this new approach. *I'll just get started, regardless of what Faith thinks.*

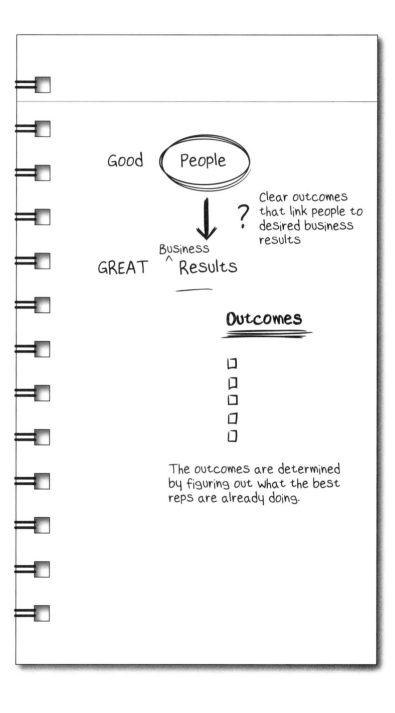

Good   People

? Clear outcomes
that link people to
desired business
results

GREAT   Business
        ^ Results

Outcomes

☐
☐
☐
☐
☐

The outcomes are determined
by figuring out what the best
reps are already doing.

CHAPTER 9

The Doubters

Marc had barely left the room with Kylie for her nightly bath and bedtime ritual when Aimee grabbed her laptop from her work satchel. As if she were in a trance, she opened the black gateway to the office, and before she realized it her mind was deep in the last ten months of sales numbers. Aimee pored over each entry of every sales rep, hoping to find obvious pointers to the standout performers. She tried to ignore the growing realization that a review of the numbers would not reveal the insights she sought. She grew frustrated as the patterns she thought would be there remained elusive.

Aimee didn't notice Marc as he quietly reentered the room but looked up when he forcefully cleared his throat. She glanced at the clock in the lower right-hand corner of the computer screen. Forty-five minutes had passed since Marc hoisted Kylie in his arms for bath time. Neither spoke.

Aimee felt obsessed with her quest to save the sales team. She couldn't shake her feeling of responsibility not only for Joe but also for the rest of the sales team and for what they meant to the success of Calara.

Marc went directly to the kitchen and poured himself a glass of water. Aimee returned her focus to the Excel spreadsheet that so far wasn't helping in her quest.

Aimee could hear Marc's distinctive footsteps on the hard-wood floor—at first, pacing in the kitchen, and then gradually getting louder as he neared the table where she was working. Without a word, Marc placed his large hand, strong and weathered from his work as a sought-after landscape architect, across the top of her laptop.

"We have to talk," he said as he slowly but firmly closed the screen on Aimee's laptop.

Aimee could feel the blood rush to her face. "I was working on that spreadsheet," she protested.

"I know," Marc said as he slid into the chair beside her. "I know."

In a stubborn gesture to resist Marc's overture, Aimee reached down to reopen her laptop. Marc's large hand again reached out and with one resolute motion firmly shut it.

"No. We have to talk. Now."

Aimee pushed herself away from the table. She stood up and faced Marc, restraining her voice so as not to wake Kylie: "You don't understand! I have to get this done. I have to get sales back on track!" Aimee's face was fully flushed. A fight at home was the last thing she needed when she was already fighting one battle at the office.

"Aimee, I know, I know, but look at you. You hardly engaged with Kylie at all tonight. You're staying up till all hours reading some stupid book—"

"You just don't understand. You have no idea of the pressure I'm under at work! I've told you about this jerk, Conroy. Can't you be a bit more understanding?"

"I want to understand, I do, but—"

"But what?"

"You haven't been the same lately!" Marc's voice rose in frustration. "You go to work early, you get home late, and then you're back to work after Kylie's in bed. Some nights you don't even make it to bed. Come on, that's not you!"

"What do you mean, that's not me? You knew what it meant for me to go back to my career, you agreed—"

"And you knew what we were both getting into when we decided to bring a child into this world."

"Keep Kylie out of this!"

"You know what I mean."

"Marc, what do you want me to do? I'm not just working for my own fulfillment. I'm working for us, for our future, too."

"I know but…I mean, everything was really good before you went back to work, and even your first couple of months back seemed to go okay." He looked down. "But now…"

Aimee was hit by the realization of what Marc was saying. "Wait, you want me to *quit my job*? Is that what you want?"

She felt the walls closing in. She believed in what she was doing. She felt it was important—not just to her but to them, to lots of people in fact. She didn't have the energy to argue with Marc. Couldn't he be more understanding and give her the space she needed to get over this hill?

"I'm not saying that, although, yes, I thought it was fine when you weren't working," he added. "I'm worried about you. I don't think I've ever seen you so stressed!"

"Marc, you know I love you—you and Kylie mean the world to me. But I have to do this. I have to turn things around for our sales team."

"I wish I could say that I understand, but I'm not sure I do."

"I just need you to bear with me; I just need to get over this hill."

"Aimee, I don't know…I just don't know right now. This kind of life—it's not working," Marc replied, with his voice now just above a whisper. "I'm going to bed. I'll see you in the morning."

Aimee sat alone at the table, placed one elbow on each side of her closed laptop, and buried her forehead in the palms of her hands. Tears welled up in her eyes. An image of Kylie effortlessly giggling popped into her head. If only Marc could see that they wanted the same results for the family: a happy home, a happy child, a secure future. The problem was, her role in achieving that result was changing, and they needed to adjust, both of them. She wished Marc could see that.

⋮

The Panera parking lot was only half full when Aimee pulled in. She was relieved to see they'd beat the lunch crowd as she pulled into a space and gathered her belongings.

She walked into the restaurant and looked around to find Joe, who was already sitting at a table, working on his iPad. *That's Joe, always connected.*

Aimee walked over and put her journal and the book down. "Hey, Joe. I figured I'd be the first one here, but no, not with you. Thanks for setting this up for me." She smiled as she sat down.

"No worries, Aimee. I was just catching up on some e-mail. Maria and Jameil are almost here. I didn't tell them much. Actually, I didn't know much to tell them. I couldn't really tell them about the internal stuff. And you were kind of cryptic about this meeting."

"That's okay, Joe. I was cryptic because I was still figuring it out myself. But now I—" Aimee stopped as Maria and Jameil walked in together and joined them.

After the greetings, Aimee said, "Let's order and grab our food before the line gets really long. Then I'll explain why I wanted to meet with all of you."

Aimee observed the way Maria, Jameil, and Joe interacted with each other and with the Panera staff. It was so natural. They treated everyone as a best friend, as though whomever they were talking to was the most important person in the place. That connection to people, she thought, might just be their "secret sauce," or the outcome they focused on. Well, she would find out soon enough.

While they ate, Aimee started to explain: "Thanks again for taking a chunk of time to get together. Here's what I wanted to talk to you about."

They mostly listened, asking only a few questions as Aimee pulled out her journal. She opened it to a page of notes she had created when she was reading "the book" (as she thought of *Exemplary Performance* now), which highlighted a distribution curve labeled with struggling, average, and top performers. She walked through what she had learned over the past week about star performers, targeted outcomes, and focused training. Those were her key themes, and she stuck to them throughout, treating the lunch meeting as a bit of a dry run for the themes of the presentation to Ian and Richard.

As she wrapped up her overview, the others were leaning forward, nodding in agreement.

"Now let's talk about what outcomes you three focus on that set you apart from your peers," Aimee said.

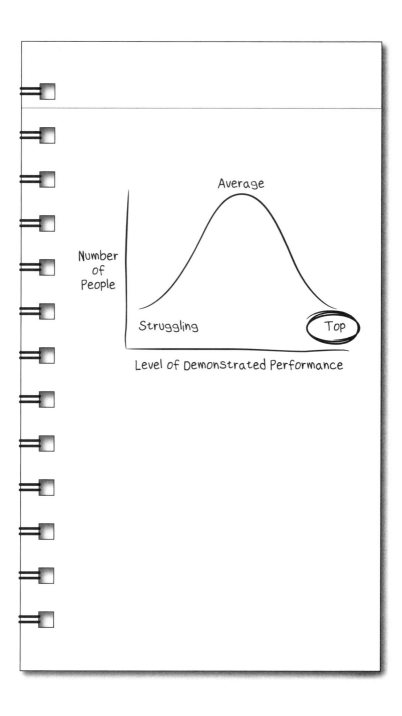

The next ninety minutes flew by as they described how they think about sales, customers, and relationships. Aimee guided the discussion, helping this team of proven top performers talk through what they did to plan for client engagements and how they approached the actual client meeting. Then she probed deeper to understand the indicators they followed to know they were on the right track.

That's when Maria opened her laptop and showed Aimee a sales spreadsheet tracking what she called "predictors."

"The corporate system tracks only activities that have already happened," Maria explained. "I need to know what's about to happen so I can get ahead of it. What can I do about what's already happened?"

Jameil and Joe smiled and looked at each other.

Aimee hadn't considered this before. "Tell me more."

"I call mine 'forecast factors,'" Joe said.

Jameil added, "My spreadsheet is called 'the bank,' because if I focus on producing those things, outcomes, as you call them, it means money in the bank!"

They all laughed. Comparing notes, they found they were all tracking many of the same elements. But each one thought he or she alone held the secret key to sales success.

Aimee stretched and shifted in the hard wooden Panera chair. She leaned over her journal and started writing. As she wrote, she announced, a little too loudly for the setting, "Well, we have our first outcome identified."

She looked up at the team and, without looking back at the page, recited what she'd jotted down:

"Outcome 1: Up-to-date planning and forecasting spreadsheet."

As Aimee flipped through the pages of her journal, reviewing the detailed notes she had captured from the team discussion, she found herself drawn to the page with the distribution curve. Its importance had grown stronger than ever.

As they got up to leave, Maria stopped Aimee: "Thanks for taking the time to listen to us. Sometimes it seems like the company has forgotten that we are real people, not just faceless human resources. But we like to know our opinions count. After all, we are the front line. We're closer to the customers than anyone else in the company."

Aimee was smiling as she pulled out of the parking lot. These were great people. They understand what needs to happen to improve the performance of the sales team. In fact, if she could clone them, Calara's short-term sales challenges would be over in no time.

Maybe we can *clone them*, Aimee mused. *If we understand what the best performers do, how they think about their work, we can teach those in the middle how to emulate that top performance. The key is focusing on the outcomes that these top performers aim for.*

She was already mentally drafting the slides for her presentation to Ian and Richard, her confidence building.

⋮

The days following the lunch seemed to fly by. The progress reports from Joe had been very encouraging. As Aimee settled behind her desk, she reflected on how much more pleasant this Monday was than the Monday just a few weeks ago. Marc had backed off on his complaints at home, and though he was still concerned about the demands of her work at Calara, he had kept quiet and not voiced his concerns. She appreciated his giving her a little space to sort out this work issue. Joe and his colleagues had really seemed to connect with her and this whole new approach. Joe's follow-up meeting with PBH Technologies had gone extremely well. He had turned a big misstep into a true victory for Calara. And maybe best of all, her encounters with Faith and Conroy had gone without a hitch.

As her computer booted up, Aimee was more confident than she had been in weeks. Of course, her computer was as slow as ever booting up. Why did it have to take so *long*?

As was her custom, the first item she checked was her e-mail in-box. One line in the list of new e-mails stuck out like a sore thumb—a meeting request from Faith. Meeting notifications usually came from Faith's administrative assistant, not directly from Faith. This one came directly from Faith, which was odd. Aimee double-clicked on the item to read the details.

> Subject: Review Aimee's objection to the sales plan
>
> Required: Martin, Aimee
>
> When: November 12
>
> Where: Conference Room 1, Boardroom
>
> Aimee, to follow up on your discussions with Ian, this is the invitation for you to present your ideas regarding the sales force. Conroy and I have already spoken, and we agree with Ian that we should give you a fair hearing.

The nasty feeling that had been remarkably absent suddenly returned in the pit of Aimee's stomach. Her thoughts raced. November 12. Faith knows that I will not have enough information to present to Richard by then. Conroy has gotten to her. She reread the message: "Review Aimee's objection...a fair hearing." What does that mean? Am I on trial?

For a moment Aimee felt paralyzed, sensing that no matter what she did, her fate and the fate of the sales force were sealed. The extent of the resistance she faced was quite evident.

There was only one thing to do: keep pedaling. Aimee was not going to quit because she faced an uphill climb.

Best to tackle the challenge head-on, she resolved. She would go directly to Conroy, but not for a confrontation. Conroy was clearly an intelligent man. She would update him on her progress over the last few weeks and offer to help him broaden the strategy for updating sales.

That's it! Aimee thought. *I'll meet Conroy halfway.*

$$\vdots$$

Aimee picked up her phone and saw Joe's name on the incoming call display. "Hello."

"Hey, Aimee," she heard Joe say. "What are you doing for lunch today?" His enthusiasm cut through Aimee's frustration about the new deadline.

"Well, getting together with you, of course. Where are you taking me?"

"How about you meet us at Factors Row in Annapolis? I want to show you what we've been working on."

"What are you talking about?"

"We'll show you at lunch. But trust me, you're going to like it! See you there at noon."

Aimee hung up, wondering what they would bring. *I hope they've pulled together some really great data. We're going to need it.*

She looked at the clock and realized she would have to hurry through these last reports to make it to Annapolis by noon. There was no way she would be late.

⋮

As the waiter refilled their coffee cups, Joe sat back and asked, "So what do you think?"

Aimee shook her head in amazement. Joe, Maria, and Jameil had gotten together and combined their tracking spreadsheets. They had agreed on a new naming convention for each of the outcomes they focused on and added success criteria to each one. The result, their Customer Relationship Worksheet, was a concise view of the five critical outcomes they agreed would lead to sales success—success that was specific to Calara.

During the discussion, Aimee copied each of the new outcomes in her journal directly under the first outcome they had detailed. She smiled as she wrote. *What a discovery process this has been—and all driven by Calara's best performers from the field.*

The list was simple yet far-reaching. Perhaps, she considered, the beauty of it was in that simplicity. She was especially pleased by the insight contained in Outcome 3: "Customer who is confident in Calara's ability to handle problems."

"I'm amazed," Aimee said. "You three have taken the concept and really run with it. These outcomes are a model of excellence for all our sales reps. Do you think the idea will work for everyone else?"

"I think we can persuade at least a few people to give it a try," Joe replied. He smiled as he added, "In fact, we've already picked two other salespeople and we're coaching them on how to use the new CRW tool to improve their results." *Typical Joe,* Aimee thought, *always operating at least a couple of steps ahead.*

- ☐ Outcome 1: Up-to-date planning and forecasting spreadsheet
- ☐ Outcome 2: Deep, trusted relationships with key client contacts
- ☐ Outcome 3: Customer who is confident in Calara's ability to handle problems
- ☐ Outcome 4: Healthy pipeline with predictable funnel progression
- ☐ Outcome 5: Current mental model of customer business and how Calara can help

Joe continued: "I think after we've captured the next level of detail, the natural next step will be to put together a little training course on how to use it. I'm really excited, Aimee. This whole outcomes idea could be a turning point for us."

This is perfect, Aimee thought. *Now all I have to do is get Conroy off the warpath.*

⋮

"Conroy, thanks for making some time this morning. I know you're busy." Aimee's words seemed to echo off the walls of Conroy's office. Conroy sat stoically behind his desk: no smile, no frown, no emotion whatsoever as Aimee confidently began to present her findings.

Aimee expected this demeanor from him so she was not fazed. She leaned forward in her chair and continued.

"I know that we have not gotten off to the best start, and I take most of the responsibility for that." Aimee hoped that a conciliatory demeanor would help crack Conroy's shell and warm him to the proposal she had in store.

She paused to gauge Conroy's reaction. Still nothing.

"As you know, things have been moving very rapidly around here and, well, I should have been more open to your ideas— given them a chance to sink in before reacting the way I did."

Aimee paused again. She detected a slight grin beginning to bring Conroy's face alive.

Interpreting the grin as a small opening, Aimee picked up the cadence and went right to her point.

"I can help you in your efforts to create a digital marketing presence for us. I know the company and I know our clients."

"Go on," Conroy finally ended his silence. His smile grew.

"Our clients are moving toward digital. But they aren't ready for a wholesale change. Parts of our message would work great in a new digital channel. I'm sure I can help sort out which parts could switch over now and what should stay conventional. Together we can fine-tune a blended message that will really resonate with them."

As Aimee paused to take a breath, Conroy leaned forward just slightly, his smile stiffened.

"All I ask, Conroy, is that you give me some leeway with the sales force." Aimee voice was strong and certain.

"What type of leeway?" Conroy responded flatly, his smile fading.

"Two things. First, I need some time to work with the reps. I need you to back off on the reduction in force you're pushing." Aimee paused.

"And second?" Conroy retorted snidely.

"Second, I'm in the midst of a revamped strategy to retrain the entire sales force. I have a new approach that I'm sure will raise the bar across the entire team. I need Joe to help me with this."

"Joe? Joe can't help you. He's not even smart enough to grab hold of the lifeline I threw his way. I offered him the chance to help me with framing the digital message, and he, like a fool, declined," Conroy said, his smile now gone.

"Look, Conroy, I've known Joe for years. He understands our clients better than anyone, and I've already talked with him and he's excited about my approach. Joe's on board. I just need you and Faith to back me and remove Joe from the list—better yet, cancel the RIF and give me the space I need to get the sales team on track."

Conroy stood and slowly walked behind Aimee to close the door to his office.

"You don't mind if we have a little heart-to-heart, do you?"

"That's why I'm here, Conroy," Aimee snapped.

Conroy remained standing after he walked back around to his side of the desk.

"Aimee, you just don't get it, do you? The train has left the station; I have both Ian and Faith on board with *my* plan. Why are you wasting all our time with the notion of retraining the sales force, making a presentation to Ian, lobbying to keep Joe?" Conroy's tone was cold.

"I have a plan that's going to work. A plan that will turn the sales team around," Aimee responded, not backing down.

"Really, Aimee. Why are you so concerned about the sales team anyway? I've offered you a position; the sooner you get on board and downsize the sales force, the better for both of us."

"No, Conroy, you don't get it. You throw away experienced people like they're bad ad copy and endanger the company's position in the marketplace by doing so. Many of the people on this sales team laid the very foundation for this company and its history of success."

"Beautiful. Really beautiful. Now I get it. You sound just like Bill."

"Bill? What's Bill got to do with this?"

"He tried to peddle that same 'people' garbage too, Aimee," Conroy responded as he strutted around to Aimee's side of the desk. He looked directly down at her as she sat stunned in her chair.

"Well, Aimee, guess what? Bill thought he could stop me, too. What makes you think that you can do what Bill couldn't?"

"What do you mean?" Aimee was getting nervous.

"I want you to listen carefully to what I am about to say. I am going to predict your future."

Aimee rolled her chair back to get out from under Conroy's stare.

"Honestly, Aimee, I don't want it to end this way, but clearly you're about to follow in the footsteps of your mentor, the mighty Bill."

Aimee's face turned beet red as she pushed herself forcefully out of her chair, creating momentum toward the closed office door.

"Oh, Aimee, one last thing: I'm going to see to it that Faith does not give you the same lucrative exit package that Bill got—and yes, you're welcome!"

Aimee barely paused long enough to catch the last element of Conroy's vendetta as she stormed out the door. When she reached the hallway, she let out a breath, working to control her emotions as she hurried toward her office. Aimee slammed the door behind her as she cleared the threshold. With the thud of the door, her anger overwhelmed her and she started shaking.

She was alone. Now she understood Bill's sudden change of course—he, too, was ambushed by Conroy. She was finished. She could do nothing more here. Marc was right: it was time for her to go back home and pour all of herself into their family and raising Kylie.

CHAPTER 10

Beating Notre Dame

Aimee rode almost twenty miles before the anger started subsiding. She was on the big ring and her highest gear, hammering along her favorite stretch of country road. Her narrow tires made a whirring sound on the road, and the crisp fall air kept her cool as the miles rolled by. Aimee realized that she needed to ease up. She could never maintain this pace for the next twenty miles. But she desperately needed to get her frustration with Conroy out of her system.

Conroy's direct assault was still ringing in her ears. She had told Doris she was taking off for the rest of the day; when she got home she grabbed her bike and headed out into the countryside to be alone. She needed a long ride to clear her head and figure out her next move. What could she do to blunt Conroy's momentum and get her plan back on track?

She turned the corner and felt the headwind. She leaned down to grab her water bottle, took a big drink, and then settled into the drops of her handlebars, shifting down a gear to maintain her pedaling cadence. Her pace was good, although maybe still a little too fast. The anger was receding and she was finally relaxing.

Maybe it was time to give up. That thought kept bubbling up. Maybe she should admit that she just wasn't ready to get back into the rough-and-tumble of the corporate world, the infighting and back-office politics. Maybe Marc was right. Maybe this was just too much of a sacrifice. She needed to get her priorities straight.

She smiled. That's not much different from what Bill told her back when she first started cycling. Get your priorities straight. Forget speed; cadence is what matters most. Keep spinning. Don't fight the pedals. Work with the bike. She glanced at her cyclometer—thirty miles down, ten to go.

She heard Bill's voice in her head: *Let other people fight their pedals. You just ride your own ride and you'll do fine.*

Ride her own ride. That's what she needed to figure out at work. What was her ride? She certainly couldn't play Conroy's game. And she didn't want to. She wanted to approach challenges her way. She knew what was right, and what Conroy was doing was certainly not right.

She heard echoes of Marc's voice when they talked about her coming back to work. "You're strong, Aim. You'll do fine." Marc. Her rock. Despite the tension lately, she knew he was always there for her. Maybe she should talk this over with him. Maybe he'd tell her what to do. Then she had to smile—she already knew what he would say: *You have great instincts. Just follow those instincts wherever they lead you and you'll be fine.*

Instincts. Her own ride. Yes, she would continue this uphill climb at Calara.

She turned the final corner heading for home. Her pedaling was still smooth, her hands were loose on the grips, and she was totally relaxed and smiling. She knew where she was headed. And she knew how to get there. Joe was enthusiastic about what he and his small team had discovered about the outcomes they must focus on. And Shafe and Coach Price swore by this outcomes focus.

Aimee pulled back into her driveway, unclipping her bike shoes from her SPD pedals as she approached the garage. Marc had just gotten out of his car and was walking around to get Kylie out of her car seat.

"Hey, Aimee. I was wondering why your car was here. What's up?" His eyes narrowed as he searched her face. "Have things gotten worse at work?"

Marc knew her too well. Aimee smiled as she leaned her bike against the garage wall and thought again about talking the whole Conroy situation over with Marc. Just then Kylie hopped out of the car, ran to her, and jumped into her arms. Aimee hugged her close.

"Nope. Just snuck out for a ride. I sure missed you two." She held Kylie and walked over to Marc. "Let's make a Kylie sandwich!" Kylie squealed and started squirming.

"No Kylie sammich! No Kylie sammich!" Kylie broke loose and ran into the yard with Marc and Aimee in hot pursuit. Marc caught Kylie, scooped her up, and fell down in the grass laughing. Aimee looked at Marc and Kylie. *Nope, nothing wrong.* She smiled and ran over to lie with them, gently hugging Kylie as she wriggled between Marc and her.

⋮

Aimee loved working with this bunch. She, Joe, Maria, and Jameil gathered around the small round table in Aimee's office. They had been working for almost two hours, but they were all just as fresh and excited as when they started.

"We've analyzed each of our outcomes and nailed down the list of key tasks and the excellence criteria associated with each.

Any final thoughts before we move on to dividing up the work ahead of us?" Aimee asked. Everyone shook their heads no.

"Okay then," she continued. "Joe, as you've mentioned before, I think what's ahead of us is pretty straightforward—not necessarily easy but straightforward," Aimee said.

They spent the next hour focusing on who would work on which parts of the plan to equip the rest of the sales reps. They knew that they would have to move quickly to complete this plan, and the tasks seemed to flow naturally among them. They would develop job aids, tools, a mini–training program, and coaching material for each outcome.

Maria took Outcome 1, "Up-to-date planning and forecasting spreadsheet."

Joe picked up Outcome 3, "Customer who is confident in Calara's ability to handle problems," and 5, "Current mental model of customer business and how Calara can help."

Jameil grabbed Outcome 2, "Deep, trusted relationships with key client contacts," and Outcome 4, "Healthy pipeline with predictable funnel progression."

The choice of who focused on which outcome fell naturally to each person based on the individual's strengths, and the banter around the table was full of teaching points and relevant scenarios. Joe revealed that of each them had already started to mentor a couple of the new and bright-eyed reps who had joined Calara in the last six months.

Aimee sat back. "Sometimes I wish I was still in the field working with customers rather than having to deal with all the internal politics."

"Yeah, right," Joe laughed. "We'd love to have you back in the field. But you're the most capable and qualified person here for navigating this craziness. In fact, Aimee, there's no one we'd rather have up here fighting for us."

Maria and Jameil smiled and nodded.

Aimee smiled. "Thanks. You make the craziness worth it. Now let's get on with it."

Joe leaned forward and circled the third outcome on their list. "This is the one I think is the most difficult but also the one I'm most excited about: 'Customer who is confident in Calara's ability to handle problems.' That's the key insight that really drives deeper relationships. And to think we've never trained our reps on it, never coached them, never helped them understand it. How could we do that to our people?"

"Because we never thought about outcomes like this," Maria said. "Aimee, this is so obvious now that we're doing it. Thank you again for taking us down this path."

"Hey, this might feel obvious to us, but a lot of people in this company still don't get it and won't unless we prove that this approach works. So how do we prove it? Here's the problem: we know this will work, but we also know it will take time—time that we may not have. What can we do to prove it now?"

"Well, I may have an idea about that," Jameil said.

"Out with it!" Maria looked at him expectantly. "Stop holding out on us!"

"Well," Jameil started again. Then he hesitated, "Okay, this may sound a little crazy, but . . . you know that Sally is chasing Accord Enterprises, right?"

"Accord?" Aimee exclaimed. "Accord is a ridiculous long shot. The probability on that deal is so low it's not on anyone's forecast list."

"But what if she uses our new approach? What difference could that make?" Maria asked. "Joe, could you mentor her and help her focus on the right outcomes?"

They all stopped and looked at each other as smiles slowly spread over each of their faces.

Jameil's smile grew the largest. "That's what makes this perfect. Accord would be a huge win, Sally is brand new, and no one is paying any attention to the deal."

Joe added, "So if we win it with our new outcomes-based approach, we win huge. If we don't, no harm, no foul. Jameil's right—it's perfect."

Aimee shook her head in amazement. "What a team! You people are fantastic. So let's get with it. Joe, you have already been coaching Sally at PBH; introduce her to the outcomes list and start working with her to penetrate Accord immediately. And keep the Accord pursuit under the radar. If we get asked, we tell the truth. But if we're not asked, we're not volunteering anything. Got it?"

"Got it," they all chimed in together while they gathered up their papers.

After they left, Aimee sat back down at the table and looked out the window. Her team had given her confidence a huge boost. But she still had doubt in the back of her mind. What was she thinking, betting everything on a new sales rep and a long-shot client? Then her smile returned. "It's perfect."

⋮

"Hi, Aimee." Conroy's head popped through the open office door.

Oh great. What does he want now? Aimee thought as she replied, "Hello, Conroy."

"Are you busy? I have someone I'd like you to meet."

Before Aimee could answer, Conroy was standing in front of her desk with a tall handsome stranger in tow. The man was impeccable, with neatly trimmed reddish-brown hair and a perfectly proportioned waist and broad shoulders, dressed in an immaculately tailored Armani suit with a red tie against a heavily starched white shirt. The way Aimee raised her eyebrows as she took in the stranger betrayed how struck she was by his physical presence.

Conroy motioned toward the stranger and said, "Aimee, I would like you to meet Bradley Johnson. He's come on board to take the reins of our new digital approach to reaching customers."

"Hi, ... Bradley, is it?"

"Yes, that's right."

"And Bradley, this is Aimee." Conroy quickly continued, "She's one of Calara's old-timers."

Aimee almost winced at being called an old-timer but Bradley gave no indication he read anything into it.

"Hi, Aimee," he spoke in a polite and flawless baritone voice. "Pleased to meet you. Conroy has told me a lot about you."

"I'm sure he has," Aimee quipped.

"I poached Bradley from ACP Consulting. He has a tremendous track record in consulting with companies on their digital strategies. Bradley is a real superstar in the space," Conroy boasted.

Conroy was beaming as he continued: "Ian is very excited to have Bradley on board. In fact, Ian called me within minutes after their first meeting, and said, 'We've got to get this guy on our team!'" Conroy took a quick breath. "Of course, I agreed immediately and told him I'd make it happen. And here we are," Conroy concluded as he glanced at Aimee as if to check her reaction.

Aimee was stone faced. "Clearly we're privileged to have you at Calara."

"Tell Aimee about the work you just completed with Global—how it changed the way they go about interacting with their customers," Conroy said to Bradley.

"Well, the bottom line is, I helped one of their major business lines segment their market and then pepper prospective clients with well-crafted digital marketing messages that resonate within that segment."

"And what were the results for Global?" Aimee asked.

"Well, they're very happy with the program and are beginning to compile the results now," Bradley answered proudly.

"I see. So the results aren't in?"

Conroy brushed past her question. "We're using Bradley's approach to move upmarket, to hook a better class of client for Calara. Bradley is really going after much more lucrative segments for us." Conroy's patronizing tone made it sound as if he were describing the ABCs and she was a preschooler.

Nonetheless, Aimee responded with genuine interest: "That's great. You mean companies like Accord Enterprises?"

Conroy deflected Aimee's question. "Is Accord one of the companies you have targeted, Bradley?"

"Sounds vaguely familiar," Bradley responded, "but I don't really get involved at that level of detail. I design the segmentation algorithm and let it do the work. Whatever companies fall out, fall out. Then they get the messages crafted specifically for that segment."

"The process is pretty slick, Aimee. This is changing everything," Conroy added as he motioned for Bradley to head out. "You must really join us sometime, Aimee. I think you'll learn a lot."

"I look forward to working with you, Aimee," Bradley said as he reached out his right hand to Aimee. As she met his hand, extended across her desk, Bradley covered their clasped hands with his left hand. "It was a pleasure meeting you," he concluded with the same mellow baritone that he opened with.

As Bradley drew back his hands, Aimee noticed the large college ring, with the unmistakable markings of Notre Dame, on his left ring finger. Aimee smiled as she responded, "Yes, I look forward to working with you also, Bradley."

As they left, two undeniable conclusions hit Aimee. First, Conroy was driving Calara to the same approach used by Global. Global! That business model was 180 degrees from Calara's. Conroy was right about one thing: Calara does need to update its approach. But try to act like Global? And he has brought in a Notre Dame stud from ACP Consulting to implement that approach here.

Second, Bradley sure seemed to know his stuff. She repeated every word of their conversation silently to herself, suddenly feeling very isolated. With the fast-approaching date for her discussion with Richard and Ian, she doubted she'd ever be able to pull together enough data to prove the value of the sales team. And now with Bradley on board, the odds on changing Ian's mind—even with Richard in the discussion—were slim and getting smaller.

⋮

Joe's unexpected drop-in the next day was a welcomed event.

"Joe, you're sure she gets it?"

"Yes, Aimee. For the third time, Sally gets it. She's clear on the outcomes. She knows the standards for each one, and we've gone through all the key tasks and interactions. In fact, she added some great ideas on ways to accelerate the process."

"Accelerate? How? Accelerate how much?"

"Aimee, trust us. We've got the field side of this transformation on track. You keep providing air cover for us and make sure we have enough time."

"I will, Joe, but how much time? The year-end forecast for the final quarter is coming in soon. I'm getting a little nervous."

"I can't know for sure, but I can tell you this much, Aimee. Sally is going from new performer to one of our best in record time. You're going to be very proud of her, especially on the Accord deal. I'm really glad that one's not on anyone's radar. It will make it that much more sweet when we bring it in."

"Really?" Aimee couldn't contain her excitement.

"Really and very soon. You can move that to the high-probability column."

"Joe, you've just made my day. Thank you, thank you. But you've got to stay close to this and make sure you've got everything covered. We can't afford any slip-ups now."

"Hah. Right, Miss Killjoy. Don't worry. I'll keep you posted."

Aimee smiled, enjoying the easy banter. *Focusing on customers is a real pleasure*, Aimee thought as Joe left her office. Her smile grew. Wouldn't it be fantastic to announce the Accord win during her discussion with Ian and Richard? That would show them. Especially Conroy and his digital expert from Notre Dame.

Thinking about Bradley, Aimee grabbed her phone and hit the button to call Shafe. "Hey, Big Brother, how're you doing?"

"Great, Aimee. What's up? You never call in the middle of the day. Anything wrong?"

"No, Shafe. Everything is great! I just wanted to congratulate you again on winning the big game."

"Thanks, Aim. It was a great game, wasn't it?"

"Yeah, it was. Hey, I was just wondering—how does it feel to beat Notre Dame?"

CHAPTER 11

Losing Faith

As Aimee turned the corner, she almost ran over Faith, who was staring at the screen of her phone, completely absorbed in an e-mail.

"Oh, hi, Faith. Didn't mean to run you over," Aimee said, swerving to avoid the collision.

"Oh, hello, Aimee. Haven't seen you in a couple of days," Faith replied.

"I know. I've been really busy. We have to catch up soon."

"Well, how about now? I've been meaning to give you a call," Faith said almost without looking up.

"I suppose," Aimee replied, caught off guard by Faith's chilly tone.

"Perfect. My office," Faith directed.

Aimee settled into the chair directly across from Faith, immediately noticing that this was the "serious" Faith sitting across from her. In an effort to mitigate whatever Faith's purpose was for the meeting, Aimee decided to try to steer the conversation and move Faith at least a step closer to supporting Aimee's ideas for helping the sales team.

"Faith, you know that I am fully committed to Calara and the team."

Without a word, Faith gave a faint nod.

"I do have some ideas that I believe can be a great complement to the digital strategy that Conroy is busy laying out. In the end, you know I want what is best for Calara."

"I know, Aimee. I was just hoping you would come on board with the digital initiative sooner."

"I see the strategy is moving ahead at full steam; I met Bradley." As soon as the words left her mouth, Aimee regretted shifting the topic. She had let the conversation move back onto Faith's turf.

"He's a great addition to the team, don't you agree." Faith's words formed a statement as opposed to a question.

"He's impressive, for sure." Aimee paused and then continued, "Faith, I have to admit that I was a bit surprised and disappointed that I was not in the loop on the decision to hire Bradley."

"It all happened very quickly, Aimee. As soon as Conroy introduced him to Ian, the decision was made."

"I see." Aimee paused, not entirely sure where to go next.

"Aimee, I've just finished running the numbers for the fourth quarter. The outlook is worse than we thought." Faith's mood grew more somber.

"When we changed our product strategy, we all knew we would be in for a rough spell during the transition," Aimee offered in defense.

"Yes, but it's more dire than we imagined; I think our only hope for the long term is to move upmarket. We need to focus on landing some big fish. We need larger customers!"

"I agree. That's one of the reasons why our strategy has to be more complex than this digital shift alone—"

Faith interrupted, "I know what you're going to say: the sales force is coming up to speed and we're going to be fine." She paused. "But we can't wait, Aimee. That's why we're betting the company on this digital transformation."

Aimee looked at the floor. So much for her thoughts on garnering Faith's support for the sales team. Now it was clear. Faith was clearly in Conroy's corner. Her upcoming pitch to Ian and Richard was her only hope to stop Conroy from dismantling the sales team.

"Conroy assures me that Bradley is the person who can make this happen and happen quickly. He's done a similar system for Global." Faith was fully in CFO mode.

"Yes, I heard."

"Conroy assures me this will work," she said. "It has to work."

"Believe me, Faith, I spend every waking minute thinking about this. I'm doing what I can."

Aimee got up to leave. She knew Calara was about to make a huge mistake but realized there was no sense making any further arguments to Faith.

"Work with Bradley. He's good," Faith added.

"I hear you, Faith. I agree, Bradley's good," she replied, thinking *but we need great.*

⋮

Aimee was reviewing the sales projections when her phone rang. "Hi, Joe. I'm taking only good news calls today. What's up?"

"Nothing but good news all the time. You know me."

"Yeah, right."

"So, Aimee—you remember that outcome we said was most difficult to produce?"

"'Customer who is confident in Calara's ability to handle problems.' Yeah, of course, I remember it. In this industry, customers know problems will crop up, and they want to know how their supplier will handle them."

"Well, you remember how we handled that problem we had in Richmond at PBH?"

"Yeah?" Aimee hesitated, uncertain where the conversation was going. "What do those two things have to do with each other?"

Joe sped up, "Well, Sally is taking the decision maker from Accord to meet with the folks at PBH. She figures that the best way to build confidence in customers about how we handle problems is for them to talk to someone who had a problem to see how well we handled it. Remember—it's all about achieving outcomes. And she's right. This is the best way to produce that outcome with potential new customers."

Aimee sat back in her chair and frowned. The risk involved in this approach was huge. Sure, Mr. Cameron and others at PBH seemed happy with how Joe and Aimee had handled the situation. But what would they say about how they got into the problem in the first place? How would Calara come across in the meeting?

"Aimee? You still there?"

"Yeah, I'm still here, Joe. I'm just processing. Are you really sure this is a smart move? I guess I can sort of see the logic. But, Joe, this is a really risky move."

"Aimee, I understand your concern. But you know I wouldn't let Sally move forward if I weren't confident about what PBH will say. We were all in agreement when we defined a confident customer as a key outcome. And besides," Joe added, "if you believe in the outcomes, and we believe in our sales team, then we have to trust them and help them produce the outcomes we defined for them."

"You're right, Joe. Of course, you're right. Just keep a close eye on the situation in case Sally needs help. And I know you're already planning to do that. So thank you."

The confidence was evident in Joe's voice: "Don't worry. I'll keep an eye on things and keep you in the loop."

Aimee hung up and leaned back in her chair, the sales projections forgotten for the moment. All she could think about was that she was letting one of her newest sales reps take the team's biggest prospect to visit a customer they had just had major problems with. What was she thinking?

Then she remembered Joe's last call about how Sally was going from new performer to star in record time. *Well, this will certainly test that theory*, Aimee thought. *A star is what we need right now.*

⋮

The Monday morning staff meeting seemed to drone on at an unbearably slow pace. Hollow words filled the air around the mahogany table. None of the departmental reports were penetrating Aimee's consciousness. She was preoccupied with thoughts of her conversation with Joe regarding the upcoming visit by Accord Enterprises to PBH Technologies. She was excited by the progress that Sally had made with her client in such a short time—and anxious about how Accord would perceive the earlier missteps that had occurred with PBH.

She considered making the Accord visit a part of her report. She knew that she should but convinced herself that her team wasn't ready with the Accord story yet, and because they weren't ready, she didn't want to risk providing Conroy any more ammunition to forward his digital-only cause. She didn't want to spring this prematurely.

"Aimee…Aimee!" Conroy repeated, jarring her from her internal monologue.

"I need you to acknowledge that you are ready to move forward with the planned reduction in staff!" Conroy barked in his typical condescending tone.

"What? I'm sorry, Conroy. I'm afraid I didn't quite get the full gist of your last comment. Could you repeat it, please?" Aimee struggled to recover and get re-engaged in the conversation.

"Well, I was simply stating that my digital team is ready to go. In fact, we've already started the program, targeting some highly desirable new clients that your sales force just is not credible with."

"And how would you know which customers our sales team is credible with, Conroy?"

"Aimee—" Conroy stopped short on his reply. "You may be right, but it's a moot point. As I announced while you were daydreaming, the time is now to move forward with the RIF. Are you prepared to take action on November thirteenth? Everything else is in place and ready to move on that date."

"What? Where did that date come from?"

"My analysis tells me that's the prime date to execute the plan. That way we can have the data all cleaned up by the end of the month and close out the year with a notable uptick. Right, Ian?"

Ian surveyed the room and carefully replied, "Based on the plan that you presented, Conroy, this seems like a reasonable date to pull the trigger. Faith, I know you've looked at the numbers side of this and according to your e-mail agree with this timing. Would you like to add anything from the financial side?"

"Wait! Just wait!" Aimee interrupted as she slowly and deliberately stood, leaning forward slightly while placing both hands firmly on the table.

"First, Conroy has not talked to me about this date. So no, I am not prepared to move forward on the thirteenth."

"Aimee, don't you remember—" Conroy was cut off midsentence as Aimee continued.

"Nor *should* I be prepared to move forward at this point. Ian, you agreed that I could have my day with you and Richard and that we would not take these drastic actions without having that discussion first."

Aimee stood up straight and turned her entire body toward Ian. Everything she had been doing with the sales team depended on that meeting with Richard.

"Ian, has that changed?" Aimee inquired with a strong and purposeful voice.

The room went silent, waiting for Ian's response.

Conroy jumped in, adding to the awkward tension. "Ian, the board meeting is on the twentieth. I can't see any reason to wait."

"Conroy, my question was directed to Ian," Aimee shot back, defending her ground.

"Yes, Aimee, I recall our conversation some weeks back," Ian finally offered, searching for a middle ground.

"And you agreed that I could present the case for preserving the sales team," Aimee added, almost forcing her words onto Ian.

"Yes, that was our agreement," Ian softly conceded. "Conroy, I would like to postpone the date for any potential RIF for the sales team until the fifteenth. Aimee, you'll have your shot to convince Richard and me. Your argument had better be sound and very persuasive. Otherwise, be prepared to move quickly with a sales team action on November fifteenth." Ian's tone left no room for either Conroy or Aimee to respond.

"Faith, please rework the numbers for the fifteenth. Now let's move on to the next topic."

As Aimee returned to her seat, she wondered if there really was time for the Accord deal to close before the deadline. She opened her journal and turned to the list of outcomes, the model of excellence. As she looked at the list, she asked herself if this model truly represented excellence. The more she looked at it, the more convinced she became. But she also realized it was going to be close. If Sally could land the Accord account, the team would be able to change the momentum toward digital-only sales. But she also realized this: without Accord, their fate was sealed.

CHAPTER 12

The Realization

A COUPLE OF WEEKS LATER, AIMEE AND MARC SAT AT THE small breakfast table by the bay window sipping their coffee. Aimee cradled her cup in her hands and said, "I can't remember the last time we enjoyed a few minutes together like this."

Marc looked at Aimee. "This was always my favorite time of the day. Even if it was just a couple of minutes."

Aimee smiled back at Marc. "Yeah, we've been running pretty fast in a lot of directions. That's why I wanted to talk for a few minutes."

Marc sat quietly waiting.

"I know my going back to work has been tough on both of us. I really thought it would be easier. I had no idea the company was changing in so many ways," Aimee said.

"Is it that bad?"

"Yeah. Worse, probably. Everything's upside down. Bill's gone. Faith has totally changed." Aimee could feel her mood sour. "And Conroy—don't even get me started on Conroy. What a jerk. And now—"

"Aimee, Aimee. Listen to yourself."

"You're right." Aimee took a deep breath. "You're right. I'm sorry. I just get so frustrated. And that's the problem."

"What do you mean?"

"The pressure is getting to me, Marc. I know it's getting to you and Kylie. The thing is, with the huge challenge in front of the sales team, I imagine it's going to get worse before it gets better—if it ever gets better. We're down to the wire on the chance to change anything. So…," Aimee said as she looked deeply into her husband's eyes, "do you think I should walk away? I'm willing to. For us. For Kylie."

"Walk away?"

"Yeah. I gave it a good try. But it's not worth hurting us or Kylie." Aimee was sincere.

"So you'd walk away now? You'd give up on all the work you've put in?"

"If you want me to, I will." Aimee watched Marc as he processed what she'd told him.

Marc stood up, walked over to the bay window, and stared outside for a long moment. Then he turned to Aimee with a determined look.

"The woman I married never gave up when the going got tough. I admit, I've had my reservations, and it's been rough at times, but I understand. You've been in an uphill battle—for yourself, the sales team, and the company. I know you; let your passion drive your perseverance. That passion and perseverance makes you who you are. Kylie has a great role model. I'm proud of you. We're right here with you all the way."

He walked over to where she sat and smiled. "So what can I do to help?"

"You just did all I could ever ask for. Thank you," Aimee said as she reached out to Marc, drawing him in with a deep hug.

⋮

As Aimee drove to the office, her phone rang, displaying Joe's name on the console. "Hey, Joe. What's up?"

"Richmond is what's up. The Accord visit to PBH went great. Sally said they hit it off really well."

"Really?" This was the break she had been looking for.

"Yes, really. She said they had some frank discussions about what we did wrong and how we handled it. Apparently, it was exactly what Accord wanted to hear."

"That's fantastic! Any obstacles to overcome?" Adrenaline spiked her voice.

"I don't think so. Sally's confident everything's going well. I'm telling you, Aimee, the new approach works—and works fast. All the success factors in the CRW are right on track—all the outcomes are on target. I swear we're going to close this deal. I think you can put the champagne on ice."

"Joe, are you serious?" Aimee was at once elated and cautious.

"Of course, I am. Just don't tell anyone yet. I predict Accord Enterprises will close right before your meeting with Richard and Ian."

"Just close it, Joe. You and Sally make sure it stays on track. I'll take care of the rest."

Aimee pressed the red phone icon to end the call. *Joe and his magic!* she thought. He'd been able to mentor Sally on how to focus on the right outcomes to quickly achieve excellence. Sally had followed Joe's model, and now they were just days away from breaking major news.

For the first time in a while, Aimee tuned in her favorite radio station and started singing along. Things were starting to look a lot brighter. Now to get that presentation together.

⋮

Aimee hardly noticed the phone ringing as she was totally engrossed in distilling her thoughts and crafting exactly the right graphic in PowerPoint to express her strategy for transforming the sales force. She glanced quickly down at her phone to the left of her computer. Faith's name illuminated the screen. *Crud, I'm on a roll and I don't really want to talk with Faith right now!*

But the ringtone was relentless, so Aimee finally conceded and picked up the phone.

"Hi, Faith."

"Hi, Aimee. Glad I caught you live."

"What's up?"

"Aimee, I'll cut right to the chase. We've canceled your presentation to Ian and Richard."

"*What?*"

"I talked with Ian, and we've decided not to waste Richard's time. Your presentation is canceled—"

"You've got to be kidding me! Faith, what's going on?"

"I recommended that we pull the plug on the discussion. It would be counterproductive to what we have to achieve. I know this is hard, but I've gone over the numbers a dozen times. We must make changes."

Aimee grew silent. She started to formulate the words to convey the progress with Accord, but before she could speak, Faith continued.

"Aimee, I am sorry. I know how much the sales team means to you—"

"Faith, wait, you don't know how close we are to a major breakthrough," Aimee pleaded.

"You are just prolonging the inevitable. Conroy and Bradley have a strong plan. The time has come to embrace it fully and not look back."

"Faith, I am begging you—give me my shot, please. I know you will see the logic behind the strategy. I just need a little more time!"

"Aimee, you know I respect you and really appreciate everything you've done for this company over the years."

Aimee offered no response as Faith droned on. "Over the years" rang in Aimee's head as the air suddenly left her lungs.

"Aimee? This transformation will go much smoother with you than without you. Listen to what I am saying, Aimee."

Aimee was no longer listening. "I'm sorry, Faith. I have to go."

"Okay, I'll stop by your office tomorrow to follow up with you," Faith said.

Aimee held her phone to her ear for several seconds after the call ended. Conroy must be behind this, she figured. Faith wouldn't do this to her without Conroy's influence.

⋮

Faith walked unannounced into Aimee's office and closed the door gently behind her. "Is now a good time to follow up on our call?" It was not really a question.

"Sure," Aimee replied, barely looking up.

"The time has come, Aimee. We must finalize the RIF list." Faith paused slightly, waiting for a reaction. "We can do it together, if you'd like." Faith handed her a single typewritten page, sat down, and looked at Aimee, waiting for her response.

Aimee sat motionless, fighting not to betray her emotions to Faith. *Just another few days,* she thought, *and Accord will come through. Then Calara can move forward with the real transformation.*

"Aimee?"

Aimee steeled herself.

"No, Faith." Aimee hoped her voice would hold together. "This is my responsibility. I'll do it."

"Are you sure? I know how hard this is for you."

"No. This is my job. How much time do I have?"

"End of the day will be fine," Faith said. "That will give us tonight and tomorrow to prepare the separation packages and do all the final calculations. There are a lot of tasks HR needs to do—"

Aimee interrupted: "I got it, Faith. I got it. You don't need to tell me all the gory details. I'll review the list and get it to you by the end of the day."

"Thanks, Aimee. And I know—" she stopped midsentence as Aimee turned her attention to the list and stopped listening. Faith slipped quietly out of the office and closed the door.

Aimee stared at the list in her hands, feeling the frustration of being so close to turning the corner. But close just didn't cut it. She put the paper down and looked at the picture on her desk of Marc and Kylie—her foundation, her motivation. Then she looked back at the list with a new clarity and the spark of purpose.

She turned to her laptop and started typing. Aimee was in the zone. This had to be done right, and she chose each word carefully.

Joe's name flashed on her phone, momentarily interrupting her thoughts. She chose to ignore Joe's call—she really couldn't face him right now—and she returned her attention to the words on the screen.

After she finished reading, rereading, and polishing, she hit the Print button and turned back to the paper on her desk. With her pen, she lined through Joe's and Sally's names. Then she wrote in large bold letters at the top of the list: "Aimee Martin."

She looked at the page and smiled, satisfied. This would buy enough time for Joe and Sally to get Accord across the finish line. Joe would then have the leeway to implement the new outcomes model and rebuild the sales force.

She grabbed the final, marked-up list off her desk and her letter of resignation from the printer, pausing only briefly to sign the letter before starting toward the door.

⋮

Aimee had made the slow climb up the single flight of stairs to Ian's office many times, but this time each step seemed filled with memories not only of the last few months but of her early years at Calara. Everything she had learned about business she had learned here—much of it from Bill. With the thought of Bill came an unsolicited commitment to find him and get his version of his sudden departure from Calara. Aimee nurtured the hope that Bill's version would somehow exonerate him. Aimee smiled with the next few steps as she imagined Marc's joy at her decision. Even though he had reassured her that he understood how much succeeding at this job meant to her, he would nonetheless welcome this decision. Of course, she was looking forward to the extra time with Kylie, too.

But it still hurt. She had given so much of herself to building this company. She didn't really expect Ian to appreciate her efforts. But Faith was a different story. Aimee truly felt betrayed by Faith's strong alignment with Conroy, with no meaningful explanation of her fervid swing in his direction. Conroy, of course, was a snake. No regrets there. He was like a cancer that had been introduced into the Calara bloodstream—one that spread rapidly to touch every aspect of the company.

Joe will be okay, her inner voice assured her. He just needs the extra time to close the Accord deal. She hoped that her decision would give Joe one last chance to turn the tide. He was resilient.

As Aimee reached the top step, she was sure handing her letter directly to Ian was her only choice. She wanted to see his face and directly gauge his reaction. It would be a small consolation for all the sweat she'd contributed to this company, but nonetheless, this was the only way to end it.

Martha, Ian's administrative assistant, was surprised to see her. "Oh, hi, Aimee."

"Hi, Martha. Is Ian in? I need to speak with him. It's important."

"He's in. He has visitors."

"Do you have any idea of how long he might be?"

"I'm not sure. He had me clear his calendar this morning. But they've been in there for a while."

"Okay, I'll come back," Aimee said, but just then the door to Ian's office rattled.

"Wait. Sounds like they're breaking up now," Martha offered.

Aimee moved away from the door to clear the way. She didn't recognize the distinguished-looking woman who was the first to walk out of Ian's office. Aimee did a double take, however, as she recognized Sally, close on the heels of the stranger.

"Sally?" Aimee blurted out, surprised, just as Ian reached the doorway.

"Speak of the devil," Ian said. "Aimee, this is Susan Cole, COO of Accord Enterprises."

"Hello, Susan, I'm Aimee Martin—" She caught herself, deciding not to add her typical, "head of sales."

Ian said to Susan, "Aimee and her team are to thank for your experience thus far with Calara."

"Then the pleasure is all mine," Susan replied. "Aimee, you should be very proud of Sally and the excellent job she's done. We're very excited about the new relationship we're about to launch. If all your people are as great as Sally, we'll be a very satisfied client."

"Yes, Sally is without a doubt one of our rising stars. Thanks for sharing that perspective." Aimee smiled as she reflected on the original question she had pondered less than a couple of months before: "How do you get great results from good people?" Sally had clearly demonstrated she is on the path to excellence.

"You are quite welcome. I apologize, but I must really get going—some pressing meetings back in the office."

Ian stepped in. "Certainly, Susan. Thank you again for visiting this morning. We're very excited about the opportunity to work with you and your team. We appreciate your trust, and I'll call you next week to check on how the initiative is progressing."

"Thanks, Ian." With that, Susan was off.

"Sally?" Aimee's intonation was packed with questions.

"I'm so sorry, Aimee. This all came together late yesterday. Joe told me that he would bring you up to speed."

So that was what Joe had been calling about this morning. Aimee had not paused long enough to call him back. "No worry, Sally. But maybe you can bring me up to speed."

"Honestly, I was very surprised at how quickly this unfolded. I have Joe to thank—Joe and the new sales tool. I feel like I've been a sponge for all that Joe has been coaching me on. His insight has proved extremely valuable."

"That's good to hear," Aimee said cautiously.

"Yeah. The whole outcomes-based approach and the sales tool he told me you developed—they're great!"

Aimee turned toward Ian and said, "Several of us have been doing some work with a new approach." Aimee was careful to acknowledge the strength of her team.

"Aimee, you should be proud," Ian said. "Sally called me late yesterday with the request from Susan to meet me. Of course, I cleared my calendar to accommodate her request."

"Thanks, Ian. It sounds like it was important and appreciated by Susan."

"She was quite explicit in relating her expectations of a business partner. We can cover that in detail later," Ian said.

He paused, carefully thinking through his next words. "Susan also volunteered two key points of her experience with us so far. First, she emphasized how insightful Sally has been in understanding Accord's needs. Best she's ever seen from an account manager."

Aimee's face lit up with a tremendous smile as she glanced at Sally, whose face bloomed into a full blush.

"And," Ian continued, "Susan also offered feedback around some of the unsolicited e-mails and blind—her word, not mine—campaign material that she and others at Accord had experienced. None of it complimentary. I assured her that would cease immediately."

"I see," Aimee said as she folded the letter in her hand in half, deciding to follow the path suddenly laid out by these new circumstances.

"Sally, would you mind giving Aimee and me a few minutes? We have some important matters to discuss."

"Absolutely, Ian. I'll send you that background information for our proposal to Accord Enterprises."

"Great, thanks." Ian turned to Aimee. "Aimee, do you have a few minutes? I'm ready to learn more about this outcomes-based sales program Sally talked about." He gestured for her to enter his office.

"Sure, Ian. I look forward to bringing you up to speed on *all* that's been happening."

CHAPTER 13

Monday Morning Staff Meeting

Aimee could hear the buzz emanating from the boardroom as she made the turn toward the Monday morning staff meeting. She glanced over at Ian, who was walking beside her but was clearly preoccupied with some element of the upcoming agenda. She looked down at the floor to prevent Ian from noticing the small smile that had formed as she thought about how nice it felt to be entering the staff meeting at Ian's side.

"Have you talked to Faith about the revised forecast?" Ian asked, as if to clear one last item from his premeeting checklist.

"Yes, we had a brief conversation. She's prepared to update the team during the meeting," Aimee responded smartly.

"Good," Ian said as they entered the conference room.

The buzz subsided as the two entered. Aimee quickly surveyed the room; the warmth of the polished mahogany table seemed to invite her to join the familiar crowd sitting around the table. Her normal seat was occupied, however.

Aimee paused slightly as Ian headed to his seat at the head of the table. Her usual spot was occupied by Bradley Johnson of the digital division, who gave her a polite smile. The only open chair left was the one to Ian's right—the one Conroy had claimed over the past two months. Aimee briefly recalled the conversation in which Ian confided that he encouraged Conroy to leave Calara.

She looked over at Faith and then, a bit reluctantly, settled into her new seat.

"Good morning, everyone," Ian opened. "We have much to cover this morning. As you all know, we have just signed the largest contract in the company's history!"

Applause and congratulations erupted from everyone gathered around the table.

"And maybe the best part of this deal is that work started last week, changing our financial picture. Faith, what's the update on the financial front?"

"I've run the numbers and am happy to report that from a financial standpoint, there is no need to continue with the planned RIF." Faith smiled as she delivered her report to another round of applause.

"And clearly from a sales-results standpoint, a RIF of the sales force would be the last thing we would want to do," Ian quickly added.

With quiet confidence, Aimee joined with everyone in the celebration. She felt a deep satisfaction that she hadn't experienced since the early days of Calara. Joe's and Sally's faces sprung to her mind.

At Ian's signal the commotion subsided, replaced with attentiveness as everyone focused on what he would say.

"I know each of you would like to join me in expressing our gratitude for Aimee's stubborn streak!" Ian smiled and was interrupted by a group chuckle. "Without her persistence, we would be having quite a different conversation this morning."

Ian turned to face Aimee. "I thank you, Aimee, for staying the course, staying true to your convictions; for keeping Calara's best interest at heart; and for always staying sure of the possibilities.

We are so grateful that you're back at Calara. We value you and appreciate your leadership."

Aimee was caught off guard by Ian's remarks. Her face turned bright red as her colleagues once again joined into a round of applause. She looked down to gather herself and found herself staring at the homemade card Marc and Kylie had given her, which she had placed in the cover of her iPad as she left home this morning. The front of the card was adorned with a collection of Kylie's random multicolor markings. They radiated a brightness that reminded Aimee of rays of sunshine. Though it wasn't visible, the brief message penned by Marc flashed in her mind: "We love you. We support your work." Aimee's eyes welled with tears as she worked to fight back her emotions so that she could raise her head to address her colleagues.

"Ahem," Aimee cleared her throat, buying a couple of extra seconds. "Ian, thank you. I truly appreciate your kind words. But the *entire sales team* has gotten us here—the team that is gathered around this table and especially the team in the field. Most of you know Joe Fabri, and we are all excited by newcomer Sally Hardesty. Joe and Sally ran point on the Accord Enterprises pursuit. They deserve the lion's share of the credit for that win."

"You're right—the team is important. Good team members form the core, but all great teams have great leaders," Ian said. "Aimee, we'll be talking a lot about what has been accomplished here, but for now, can you give us a breakdown of what led to this success?"

"More than happy to, Ian," Aimee replied with a broad smile. She strode to the whiteboard at the front of the room and in thick letters wrote "TOPS" vertically down the board.

She turned back to her colleagues. "The TOPS model provides a straightforward approach to ensure that people who are filling critical roles throughout the organization are equipped to reliably and predictably meet or exceed the standards of excellence required to deliver Calara's business strategy."

Aimee then filled in around the letters:

Identify **T**op performers

Uncover **O**utcomes they focus on

Equip **P**eople to produce these outcomes

Coach for **S**uccess

Aimee briefly explained each of the steps in the approach.

When she finished, Ian stood up and walked over next to Aimee and announced, "This new approach and the obvious impact it's already had is just one of the reasons why I am happy to announce your appointment as vice president of sales and marketing."

The room once again responded with congratulations and applause.

"Thank you, Ian. I'm honored. I am honored to be a part of this team, and I am honored to serve Calara," Aimee said earnestly.

Ian continued with his praise and then shifted the meeting to get an update from the vice president of operations. Aimee's thoughts drifted and she lost focus on the dialogue in the room. She couldn't wait to talk with Joe. Her first act as a vice president would be to create a director of sales force readiness position and promote Joe into that role. He could fully build out the program he started with Sally and then integrate online efforts to support the outcomes his team identifies.

The Monday morning meeting faded further into the background as Aimee opened her journal to the page where she had

OUTCOMES THINKING

- ☐ Outcome 1: Up-to-date planning and forecasting spreadsheet
- ☐ Outcome 2: Deep, trusted relationships with key client contacts
- ☐ Outcome 3: Customer who is confident in Calara's ability to handle problems
- ☐ Outcome 4: Healthy pipeline with predictable funnel progression
- ☐ Outcome 5: Current mental model of customer business and how Calara can help

written the list of outcomes. She wrote "Outcomes Thinking" in bold letters across the top of the page. She glanced at the list beneath the new title.

The list brings amazing clarity to the job of the sales rep, Aimee affirmed. The training activities developed by the team were undeniably effective—and were only the beginning. Joe had gone beyond just training with Sally; he had coached her specifically on her ability to produce this list of outcomes. That targeted coaching is what really drove home the model.

Now that she had a clear model of the role sales reps play, Aimee could see Calara using these outcomes to guide the hiring and interview process. The leverage was incredible, Aimee thought as she wrote:

Leverage Outcomes:

- Hire those who fit the model role

- Equip people to produce the outcomes

- Coach for excellence

- Measure for sustained performance improvement

When the team created the Outcomes Thinking list, it seemed at first like just a good idea to provide immediate help to the sales team. These ideas, however, could be leveraged to not only help individuals learn but also serve as the foundation for how a company could make a fundamental shift and move the performance of an entire workforce. Aimee underlined "Leverage" because the notion added new relevance to the list of outcomes above it.

The rustle of paper and chairs brought Aimee's attention back to the room, where the meeting was over. Individual congratulations came her way as the team ambled out and on to the business

OUTCOMES THINKING

- ☐ Outcome 1: Up-to-date planning and forecasting spreadsheet
- ☐ Outcome 2: Deep, trusted relationships with key client contacts
- ☐ Outcome 3: Customer who is confident in Calara's ability to handle problems
- ☐ Outcome 4: Healthy pipeline with predictable funnel progression
- ☐ Outcome 5: Current mental model of customer business and how Calara can help

LEVERAGE OUTCOMES:

- Hire those who fit the model role
- Equip people to produce the outcomes
- Coach for excellence
- Measure for sustained performance improvement

of the day. As the last congratulations had been issued, Aimee's thoughts turned to her arrival home tonight. *I may have to leave a little early this afternoon to make sure I'm home on time and to sneak in a celebratory bike ride.*

Aimee hurried from the room and down the hallway to find Joe. As she turned the first corner, the "Navy Blue and Gold" ringtone she had assigned to her brother blasted from her phone. She looked down to catch the confirming name on the screen, Shafe.

"Oh, hi, Bro," Aimee began confidently, "I've been wanting to connect with you! We need to compare notes on the Outcomes Thinking model you introduced to me. I've got some refinements to tell you about."

The TOPS Model

We don't lack for "doing" in today's organizations. What is seldom present, however, is a focus on the elements that make a real impact. Focus settles the mind on a purposeful objective. It allows people to perform in a manner that delivers real impact. That impact comes from the outcomes people produce through their work. Those outcomes are what really matter—the tangible things that can be assessed and measured.

For leaders who need to ensure that those in critical roles are having the impact envisioned in the organization's business strategy, a basic understanding of the outcomes approach is a must. Armed with that understanding, they can ensure that proper resources are dedicated to create the impact required of the frontline workers.

For anyone in the business of improving people's performance or executing new or revised strategies, the outcomes focus represents a new mental model for building worker performance. This new model does not require a radical shift but rather a mere quarter turn in how we think about the task of improving performance. It moves beyond the questions of what people need to know, what skills they need to master, and what capabilities they should have to instead simply and powerfully focus on a new question: what outcomes do top performers produce?

This new thinking doesn't replace other important organizational elements such as good leadership, technology systems, aligned incentive systems, and the hiring of good people. Instead, the outcomes approach will magnify the impact of each of these elements. In an ideal situation, leadership, technology, incentives, and hiring, as well as programs to equip performers, will all align to help the workforce produce the right outcomes on a daily, weekly, and monthly basis. When present, this alignment assures the type of impact envisioned during the crafting of the business strategy.

This quarter turn in thinking requires change. Achieving meaningful change is always a journey. To be successful, we have to adopt the type of mental and emotional fortitude exhibited by Aimee. Her quest was fraught with external obstacles and internal self-doubt. It was not an easy journey, but she was driven by what she intuitively knew to be a better way. If business impact is your goal, we urge you to shift your focus to outcomes and begin your quest today. Just like Aimee, you can create real game changers in your organization as well as become one yourself.

For good leaders in any business, Aimee's story will resonate with the leadership and development ideas they know to be true. Like Aimee, however, too often they do not have the tools or framework to act on these ideas. The TOPS Model that Aimee arrives at by the end of the story provides a framework to discover and leverage the practices and thought processes of your organization's very best performers. Indeed, it provides a straightforward method to uncover and focus on the outcomes that matter and drive the realization of your business strategy.

The TOPS Model consists of four phases:

Identify **T**op performers

Uncover **O**utcomes they focus on

Equip **P**eople to produce these outcomes

Coach for **S**uccess

Each phase is introduced below. A detailed checklist is also provided as a resource to guide your journey to uncover and focus on what matters. In addition, frequently asked questions about the model are included at the end of this appendix.

Identify **T**op Performers

Who are your top performers? In our experience, first-blush answers to this question are seldom right. Defining top performance requires a clear understanding of the organization or business strategy. When we think about what we're ultimately trying to accomplish, the answer is often not obvious. Sales organizations might have many answers. Are we trying to build long-lasting relationships that generate predictable revenue? Are sales of new products better than sales of existing ones? Is territory growth and penetration the most valuable measure of success? We've seen all those answers and more. And for any given organization, the "right" answer will vary. You need to think clearly about exactly what you are trying to accomplish before setting about to improve the results.

The next challenge is to identify those people who are already making an impact. Clearly, not everyone performs at the same level. For any distinct role, be it a lineman on a football team, a salesperson, or a lab technician, some people excel, some are solid "average" performers, and others struggle. The better performers typically think about the work differently from others in a way that allows them to focus on the few key factors that really matter. Often they aren't even consciously aware of their different, and better, focus. To them, it's natural. But to others, especially the average performers, that mental model is elusive. Like the exemplars, they are working hard and trying to excel. Unfortunately, they are often working hard at the wrong tasks. Therefore, the results they produce don't make as much of an impact. So no matter how hard they work, they simply can't have the same impact as the exemplars we seek. This is a truth worth repeating: working harder to produce the wrong outcomes simply will not produce the results we seek.

Those top performers we search for are not necessarily those with the most seniority, those with the longest tenure, or even those with the most potential or capability to perform. Finding people who have great potential but are simply not performing to expectations is quite common. Instead, we seek to identify those who are currently producing the most impact aligned to the desired business strategy. They alone are the top performers.

Uncover Outcomes They Focus On

Thinking about a role and the work accomplished by someone in that role in terms of the outcomes produced is new and different. New and different is often challenging. Instead of outcomes, people usually think about the list of tasks they do or the capabilities they bring to their work or even the competencies they have. While those items are all important, they should be considered only in the context of the outcomes produced that add value to the organization. The first priority must be to discover the right outcomes. These are the outcomes that the top performers produce routinely while thinking that others in the role certainly produce similar outcomes of value.

The top performers have truly become unconsciously competent. To break through this layer of unconscious competence, we must use proven methods of observation and interviewing to discover—or perhaps, more accurately, to uncover—the true elements that make their ability to produce exemplary.

Equip People to Produce These Outcomes

No matter our business or occupation, we would all like to hire and work alongside the most talented people in our chosen field. Many organizations take this approach to the extreme and seek to hire only the most "talented" people. As the sole strategy for individual and organizational performance, however, this approach has major flaws. Even if we assume our organization will get its fair share of the available natural talent, that won't be enough to run and grow the business with excellent and predictable results. It turns out that Geoff Colvin was right in his book on this topic, *Talent Is Overrated*.

We are not suggesting that organizations stop trying to recruit the best and brightest; we're simply acknowledging that such efforts can never be enough. We strongly advocate, as a modern-day necessity, developing robust systems to grow and equip our own talent. For our workforce to deliver the desired impact, we must create the means whereby *good people can produce* great *results*. Using the outcomes uncovered from top performers as the basis for a robust development system is both powerful and efficient—powerful because it focuses development on the things that matter and efficient because it eliminates wasted effort on things that don't matter.

Coach for Success

Initial learning is not enough to embed true, sustained performance in an organization. Businesses have to take a page from the playbook of sports teams: they must coach for success. This doesn't mean occasional sessions of encouragement. Instead, it means persistent attention to fundamentals, details, and results. This type of coaching provides focused guidance on how to produce the outcomes required. When you identify what top performers focus on, what tasks they do to produce the desired outcomes, how they measure what they produce, and what resources they use to help them, you draw an explicit map to top performance, one that can be easily communicated and replicated through an outcomes-based coaching model.

$$\vdots$$

Additional guidance for each of these phases is provided in the checklist that follows. This checklist provides a framework for any organization to begin to uncover and truly leverage the outcomes produced by their top performers.

TOPS Checklist

The TOPS Checklist is designed to help you begin your first game-changing project. It will walk you through a proven step-by-step approach to identify the vital outcomes necessary to model top performance, whether you are improving the performance of a sales force, shoring up customer support centers, or creating new and consistent standards of excellence for your first-line supervisors. This checklist is divided into four phases, each one aligned with a major element in the TOPS Model:

- Phase 1: Identify *Top* performers
- Phase 2: Uncover *Outcomes* they focus on
- Phase 3: Equip *People* to produce these outcomes
- Phase 4: Coach for *Success*

*Phase 1: Identify **T**op Performers*

☐ **Develop a clear understanding of the organization's business strategy and goals.**

Businesses and organizations are dynamic. If you are a business leader, you need to clearly communicate your strategy. If you are someone in a position to support the leader, you must clearly understand and align with the leader's strategy. Examples of specific strategies include the following:

- Improve sales force performance to drive an increase in sales
- Execute a new product or customer strategy
- Implement an omnichannel retail experience
- Improve customer loyalty or "stickiness"
- Reduce the number of errors in complex customer relationships
- Improve customer satisfaction scores

You must understand what the business wants or needs to accomplish and how you will measure success. What metric will be used to measure overall progress or improvement in a specific area?

Enter the business strategy and the organizational metric for your project:

Business strategy	Organizational metric

☐ **Identify two or three roles critical to achieving the business strategy and score each of the roles from 1 to 3 on the following characteristics:**

- *Impact:* Impact on the desired business strategy
- *Variability:* Variability within the role
- *Population:* Population of performers assigned to the role
- *Error effect:* Consequence of error committed by performers
- *Turnover:* Turnover within the role

Enter and score (from 1 to 3) the roles under consideration (1 equals low/small/minor, 2 equals medium, and 3 equals high/large/major):

Role	Impact	Variability	Population	Error effect	Turnover	Total Impact Score

☐ **Based on the sum of the scores, select the most critical role to focus on during your project.**

Enter the role with the highest Total Impact Score from the previous table:

Selected role

☐ **For the role you've selected, identify, by name, top performers who are currently performing with the desired level of excellence or who come closest to the expectation.**

In an ideal world there would be a single superstar performer to model. That situation is rare. Usually, the "model performer" will be a composite of several people, each of whom is very good at some aspect of the role. You will learn unique perspectives for top performance from each individual identified.

Enter the names of the top performers you have identified and the reason for each person's selection:

Top performer	Reason for selection

Phase 2: Uncover **Outcomes** They Focus On

☐ Decide on the most appropriate data-gathering techniques. Select from interviewing, direct observations, and data analysis.

When possible, direct observations should be used in conjunction with interviewing and data analysis. At a minimum, an interview of each top performer must be conducted. Additional guidance for conducting observations and interviews is provided in the next several checklist items.

Enter specific reasons to use or not to use each technique and decide on the technique's appropriateness:

Data-gathering technique	Reasons to use and not to use	Use/ don't use
Interviewing		
Observations		
Data analysis		

☐ **Evaluate the potential to observe top performers doing their work. Factors to consider in deciding whether or not to observe performers include the following:**

- *Safety:* Will observing the performers cause safety concerns for the performer or observer?

- *Social impact:* Will the performers be able to do their work while being observed?

- *Environment:* Will observers be able to see the performers working?

- *Business impact:* Will observing the performers impact business results?

Enter the considerations for conducting observations:

Factor	Considerations	Okay or not?
Safety		
Social impact		
Environment		
Business impact		

For this group of top performers, will you conduct observations? If yes, refer to the next two checklist items. If not, skip the next two checklist items.

☐ **Develop a checklist for observing performers that probes the areas listed below.**

Top performers often take the flow of their work for granted. They are "unconscious experts." Watch carefully for shortcuts they take, personal job aids they use, and how they overcome obstacles they encounter. Items to include on your checklist might include the following:

- What initiated each work activity?
- What aids or cheat sheets were used?
- What assistance was sought?
- How were results evaluated?
- What obstacles were encountered? How was each overcome?

☐ **Observe top performers doing their work.**

Remember that you are observing to learn, not to help or to manage the performer. Your attitude and demeanor will play a large part in determining the value of the data you collect. If you are perceived by the performers to be genuinely interested in learning what they do and how they do it, you are likely to gather rich, contextual data. The most helpful technique for doing this is to put yourself into a mode where you are trying to learn how to do the job yourself.

A good way to begin the conversation with the person you observe is to acknowledge his or her reputation as a top performer. For example, you might say, "You have been identified for this process because of your demonstrated ability to perform this role at the highest level. Through discussion and observation, I would like to understand how you approach the job and what specifically leads to your success."

☐ **Develop a list of open-ended interview questions customized for the role under consideration.**
The purpose of the interview is to learn how top performers approach their work and to uncover any outcomes they produce that help them excel. The interview should take the form of an extended conversation focusing on their work and specific accomplishments that they feel produce value for the organization. The prepared questions should serve as a springboard to a more in-depth conversation. Consider the following examples when developing your question list:

- Walk through a day in your work life. What do you do? How do you know when to do it? Whom do you work with to do it?

- How do you know how well you are doing? What indicators do you use? Do you have a way of predicting how the work is going?

- What are the five to seven major outcomes (things you produce) that you focus on in your job?

- How did you learn how to produce each of those outcomes well?

☐ **Plan and conduct interviews with all of the top performers identified above.**

☐ **Gather and analyze any available data about the role and the desired level of performance. Useful data might include call statistics, customer satisfaction surveys, and business results comparing top and average performers.**

☐ **Synthesize the data gathered from the interviews and observations into a list of outcomes along with the key tasks that top performers do to produce those outcomes.** This process is best done iteratively, particularly if multiple people were involved in the data collection. The final outcome list will be a composite of outcomes produced by several different top performers. As you list outcomes, continually ask, if someone produced these things and nothing else, would he or she be successful in this role? For the key tasks necessary to produce each outcome, look for the key factors that set top performers apart from others in the role. We refer to this combination of outcomes and key tasks as a TOPS Profile.

Based on your findings, list the major outcomes and associated key tasks:

Outcome	Key tasks
Outcome 1	Key task 1a
	Key task 1b
	Key task 1c
Outcome 2	Key task 2a
	Key task 2b
	Key task 2c
Outcome 3	Key task 3a
	Key task 3b
	Key task 3c

Phase 3: Equip People to Produce These Outcomes

☐ **Develop a learning program to teach people how to produce each of the outcomes to the desired standard of excellence.**

Learning programs can take many forms, depending on the experience level of the audience, the complexity of the tasks required to produce the desired outcomes, the time and environment available for learning, and numerous other factors. The key to a successful learning program in the TOPS Model is to focus each element of the program on one or more of the major outcomes.

In many companies, learning is a specialty function, so developing a TOPS learning program may require assistance from learning professionals. The most successful programs are those that combine different modalities for learning into a package that closely resembles the actual job.

List the learning elements required to train someone to produce each outcome:

Outcome	Key elements to learn
Outcome 1	Learning element 1a
	Learning element 1b
	Learning element 1c
Outcome 2	Learning element 2a
	Learning element 2b
	Learning element 2c
Outcome 3	Learning element 3a
	Learning element 3b
	Learning element 3c

Phase 4: Coach for Success

☐ **Develop coaching guides to assess and improve production of each of the outcomes.**

Many books have been written on methods and techniques to coach performers in the workplace. There is power in coupling great coaching techniques with a focus on specific, objective outcomes that can be measured and improved. Regardless of the techniques being used by your organization, outcomes-based coaching is an essential ingredient for driving performance across the critical roles in an organization. The TOPS Model will enable first-line supervisors to coach individuals toward the accomplishment of each outcome developed and to provide insights and action plans tailored to specific performance gaps. To help facilitate this, specific coaching guidance, which cross-references best practices, material from the learning program, and external courses or experiences should be developed for each outcome used to define the role.

List the indicators of success and key coaching points to be included in coaching guidance for each outcome:

Outcome	Indicators of success	Coaching elements
Outcome 1		
Outcome 2		
Outcome 3		

Frequently Asked Questions Regarding the TOPS Model

1. How does the focus on outcomes and the execution of the TOPS Model impact business results?

Our experience is that the most significant impacts to a business's bottom line typically result from improvements in the performance of people in critical roles. Improving the performance of "the moveable middle" in these roles and closing the gap between top and average performers yields significant impact.

When compared to top performers, average performers have a lot of room for improvement. Simply closing a portion of the gap between the average and top performers creates much better business results. And since some people are already performing at the top level, it's not a leap of faith to expect new levels of performance across the entire role population.

The math of big numbers works to great advantage when outcomes are leveraged. Assume 20 percent of the workers are in the top performing group, 20 percent in the struggling group, and 60 percent in the average group—the moveable middle. Shifting the performance of the 60 percent in the moveable middle in any critical role by just a few percentage points will often transform an organization. In a sales force of one hundred sales reps, for example, improving the revenue generation of the sixty average performers by as little as 5 percent will yield a major impact to both the top and bottom line of the organization. Our experience is that improvements on the order of 10–15 percent on the part of average performers are well within expectations.

2. Can the TOPS Model be applied to roles other than sales?

Yes. While sales roles are often the focus of business improvement efforts, the TOPS Model applies to any role that is critical to the success of the organization. Roles that have yielded significant business impact include the following:

- Customer service or call center personnel
- Operations and maintenance staff
- Sales executives and product sales engineers
- Account managers
- High-net-worth financial advisors
- Healthcare workers
- Team leaders and other frontline supervisors
- IT professionals

3. *What is the leader's role in developing an outcomes-based mind-set in the organization?*

Leaders must establish and communicate clear business goals that serve as organizational and individual targets for performance. They must also visibly and enthusiastically support the diagnostic work required to identify the critical roles and the outcomes necessary to achieve the stated business goals.

Once the roles and outcomes have been identified, the leaders' role shifts to sponsoring the recommended actions and interventions that result from a TOPS effort.

4. *What is the most difficult aspect of implementing the TOPS Model?*

Change management is difficult. The TOPS Model represents a new way of thinking and can result in significant changes in how frontline workers are equipped, coached, and hired. Desires to implement the TOPS Model compete with the ongoing clutter of multiple strategic initiatives, and because an outcomes-based approach requires a new way of thinking, it can be met with resistance.

One way that resistance manifests itself is in people's refusal to provide access to frontline performers to gather the necessary data. Usual objections point to how busy the frontline performers are and how important it is that they not be disturbed. Our experience has been that top performers welcome the opportunity to participate in an improvement effort and willingly make themselves available for the TOPS analysis.

Regardless of the source of the resistance to change, leaders need to stay the course and "keep pedaling" through each peak and valley encountered on the journey to focus on what matters.

5. *Can the TOPS Model be used when performance is subpar across the entire population of performers in a role?*

Yes. Our experience is that there are always top performers, even when the overall performance for the role is subpar. In these cases, it can be even more important to use the TOPS Model to uncover the outcomes required to establish a clear standard of excellence, which can then be used as a basis for learning and coaching programs.

6. *Can the TOPS Model be used to assist in the execution of strategic initiatives?*

Yes. One key element in the successful deployment of new strategies is developing a clear understanding of changes in the outcomes required of people in critical roles. Using the TOPS Model to clearly link required changes in performance to desired business impacts of the initiative will highlight new learning and coaching required and changes in processes or tasks needed to improve the likelihood of initiative success.

7. *What is the fundamental product created during a TOPS initiative?*

A TOPS initiative generates a blueprint for what a successful performer must produce on the job. This blueprint lists the critical outcomes and the key tasks required to achieve the desired standard of excellence and is referred to as a TOPS Profile.

In simplest terms, a TOPS Profile describes how top performers view and execute their role.

8. *What's next after I understand the outcomes? What do I do with the list of outcomes once I have it? How do I leverage the outcomes?*

With a TOPS Profile in hand, you can hire, train, assess, and coach people based on the outcomes identified. With the outcomes as a baseline, you will be able to establish a positive-feedback loop: hire people better suited to the role, train them more effectively and efficiently, coach them to higher performance, and, as a result, understand the role more clearly.

9. *Can TOPS Profiles be used to develop a curriculum?*

Yes. TOPS Profiles are frequently used to identify design points for curricula. Designers can focus on the identified outcomes and tasks to build comprehensive programs for new hires or enhanced programs to boost incumbent performance. The outcomes in a TOPS Profile provide both a focus on the skills and knowledge needed and a filter to remove modules for teaching skills and knowledge that don't contribute to the production of the identified outcomes.

10. *How are TOPS Profiles used in coaching?*

Most coaching programs emphasize coaching techniques but fail to provide a clear picture of what individual success looks like in the role. One of the primary values of defining roles in terms of outcomes is that it provides objective targets for coaches and performers. Proper coaching techniques are still essential. But combined with a clear target, those techniques take on a new level of effectiveness and power.

11. Can TOPS Profiles be used as part of job design?

Yes. When the list of outcomes is evaluated, job designs can be significantly improved and successful teaming approaches can be developed. For example, a large number of outcomes (more than seven to nine) could mean the job is too broad and not focused on what really matters to the organization. A small number of outcomes (fewer than three to four) could mean the job is too narrow to sufficiently challenge and engage performers.

12. How can TOPS Profiles be used in hiring?

TOPS Profiles are often used in the creation of both hiring guides and interview guides. Asking candidates if they have ever produced the specified outcomes or how they would approach producing such outcomes provides a better picture of the candidates' potential for excellence. As a corollary, candidates who see a list of TOPS outcomes better understand the expectations of the role and are more likely to self-select either into or out of the role.

13. What is the difference between a TOPS Profile and a competency profile?

Competency profiles can help identify the right person for a given role by assessing minimal aptitudes, potential abilities, or other traits present in candidates. A competency profile, however, is of little help to a person actually in the role. A TOPS Profile helps each person in the role focus his or her efforts on the specific work required to produce the outcomes necessary for success in the role.

14. Why is it important to start the process by identifying business goals?

The first and most important step in any improvement process is to understand the goal and clearly define how the desired improvement will be measured. Without that definition, communicating and measuring success are impossible. With the goal and measurement clearly defined, identifying which people are performing well and making positive contributions to the business becomes possible. These are the top performers who should be the targets of a TOPS initiative.

15. How do I select top performers?

Select those performers you want to "clone"—those you wish were handling all the difficult tasks and difficult client situations or responding to all the trouble spots. In other words, select those who contribute most to the desired business results.

Understanding whom not to select is just as important. Do not necessarily select those with the longest tenure or the most seniority and do not select those who used to be in the role (for example, managers), regardless of how good they might have been.

16. How do I differentiate between tasks and outcomes?

Outcomes are the things that people produce as a result of performing tasks. Outcomes are things that are left behind when the performer leaves the room, and they can be counted and objectively evaluated against a standard of excellence. Outcomes are nouns; tasks begin with verbs.

Phrasing outcomes as nouns is important because nouns stimulate performers to think and respond to questions about their work in terms of accomplishments or results, which in turn leads to new and more powerful insights.

Acknowledgments

WHEN WRITING ACKNOWLEDGMENTS, THE MAJOR RISK IS ONE of omission. In a book like this, that risk is even more heightened since we have been the beneficiaries of the work and experience of many people who have taught us along the way. One such person worth special mention is Dr. Paul Elliott, coauthor of *Exemplary Performance*, a longtime colleague and close friend.

We have been privileged to work with many outstanding people in the course of our careers. Of particular note are our colleagues at both RWD Technologies and GP Strategies Corporation. We have learned much from each of them. Thank you.

Thank you also to our editors, Samantha Dunn and Sharon Goldinger, whose editing suggestions were always on target.

Our earliest editors, critics, and encouragers were our wives. They read the story, made critical suggestions, and patiently listened to far too many discussions and debates that helped shape the story. We cannot thank you enough.

And, of course, we would be remiss not to thank our clients. From them we both gained experience and honed the techniques and processes that form the basis of Outcomes Thinking. They are the true New Game Changers. Thank you all.

About the Authors

Greg Long is a recognized thought leader in the area of performance improvement, focusing on how improvements in individual performance help organizations realize improved business results. He serves as a vice president of organizational excellence for the global consulting organization GP Strategies Corporation.

After graduating from the US Naval Academy with a degree in aerospace engineering in 1978, Greg served in the Civil Engineer Corps, working in the fields of construction and facilities management. During his time in the Navy, he began to develop his understanding of human performance, organizational readiness, and the value of execution excellence.

After completing his graduate work at Texas A&M University, Greg spent three years teaching engineering on the faculty of the US Naval Academy, learning the craft of translating complex information into practical language. That craft helped launch his consulting career.

Greg now has over twenty-five years' experience providing consulting services to numerous firms around the globe. His work has focused on improving organizational and individual performance through conceptualizing, designing, and developing strategic solutions for various communities. His programs have resulted in dramatic, measurable increases in both business results and individual performance measures.

Working with performers in various roles, including executives, salespeople, account managers, and manufacturing operations and maintenance technicians, Greg has developed a penchant for helping organizations close the gap in performance between top performers and average performers. He and Butler Newman have worked to refine their methods into a practical approach for discovering and documenting both the differences that define performance excellence and developing programs to drive improvements.

That approach has been used to great advantage in numerous industries, including aerospace, pharmaceutical, financial, retail, insurance, and other complex, knowledge-based environments where excellent frontline performance is crucial.

Greg has authored numerous articles and presentations for national and international conferences and journals. He is a sought-after speaker for groups large and small.

He and his wife live in Annapolis, Maryland, where they enjoy bicycling, sailing, and other outdoor activities.

⋮

Butler Newman is a recognized leader in the field of organizational performance, consulting with business and learning leaders to ensure top performance in roles critical to their organizations' success. He has published multiple articles on the topic, and as vice president of performance excellence, Butler leads the Organizational Excellence practice for the global consulting organization GP Strategies Corporation.

He began his career as an officer in the US Navy. A 1979 graduate of the US Naval Academy, Butler served in the engineering department of the top ship in the Navy's Atlantic Fleet, where he received his Naval Nuclear Engineer Certification and later led the training of new recruits through their initial nuclear qualification process at the Navy's shore-based training facility.

Since leaving the Navy, Butler has consulted with numerous organizations on both individual and organization performance improvement initiatives, including Fortune 100 companies across diverse industries such as automotive, consumer products, retail, financial, telecommunications, healthcare, and pharmaceutical. He has led regional and global initiatives in the United States, United Kingdom, Netherlands, South Africa, and Indonesia.

Butler and Greg Long have worked together across multiple aspects of organizational improvement for over twenty-five years. They have collaborated many times to meet the specific needs of their clients and have extended that collaboration to produce this, their first book.

In addition to writing and working with his clients, Butler loves speaking to business and learning leaders on what it takes to produce top performance in their organizations. His first area of emphasis is always the same: the frontline performers. His topics include role clarity, coaching, equipping frontline supervisors and their teams, and building high-performance teams.

Butler enjoys spending time at home and traveling with his wife of thirty-four years and their two sons. He keeps a full schedule visiting clients, honing his amateur photography skills, watching and analyzing college football, and deepening his understanding on the secrets of top performers across various disciplines.